I0815426

COOKIES

THE CLASSICS

 • 13-Digit ISBN: 978-1-40035-199-2 • 10-Digit ISBN: 978-1-40035-199-5 • This book may be ordered by mail from the publisher. Please include $5.99 for postage and handling. Please support your local bookseller first! • Books published by Cider Mill Press Book Publishers are available at special discounts for bulk purchases in the United States by corporations, institutions, and other organizations. For more information, please contact the publisher. • Cider Mill Press Book Publishers • "Where good books are ready for press" • 501 Nelson Place • Nashville, Tennessee 37214, USA • cidermillpress.com • HarperCollins Publishers, Macken House, 39/40 Mayor Street Upper, Dublin 1, D01 C9W8, Ireland (https://www.harpercollins.com) • Typography: Sofia Pro, Granville • Image Credits: Pages 11, 12, 13, 17, 20–21, 26, 41,44, 48–49, 50, 52, 66–67, 80–81, 92, 96, 100, 106–107, 114–115, 124–125, 128–129, 132–133, 140, 162, 184, 190, 208, 210, 222–223, 250, 268, 272–273, 274, 278–279, 284, 288–289, 290, 293, 302, 310, 312–313, 326, 334, 340, 342–344, and 348 used under official license from Shutterstock. Pages 4–5, 7, 8, 14–15, 16, 22, 24, 28, 38, 70, 88, 112, 118, 120, 158–159, 160, 174–189, 194, 204, 214, 230, 234, 236, 238, 240–241, 258, 260, 264, 305, 308, 314, 318, 320, 328, and 337 courtesy of Unsplash. Page 330 courtesy of Cider Mill Press. All other images used under official license from StockFood. • Printed in Malaysia • 25 26 27 28 29 PJM 5 4 3 2 1 • First Edition

COOKIES

THE CLASSICS

CONTENTS

INTRODUCTION

More than any other confection, cookies reside in the memory, in the mind. Thoughts of the winter holidays are inevitably marked by the sight of cookies piled high on a tiered stand, proudly displaying the bounty from a recent cookie swap. The warm feeling of an afternoon spent making drop cookies with a loved one, where we traded turns licking the spoon, never leaves us. Instinctually, upon encountering the alluring fragrance of freshly made chocolate chip cookies, we tap into our inner cat burglar, sneaking into the kitchen to pilfer a cookie and bask in its sumptuous warmth.

What, you may be wondering, can explain this powerful hold on our hearts, minds, and memories?

As with any massively potent entity, it is not because of one specific thing. Instead, it is through the accumulation of many factors, which combine to form a considerable mass that leaves a deep, lasting impression when encountered.

The primary pieces of this powerful conglomerate are the senses, the most important of which is smell. To put it plainly: while baked goods are revered for their ability to positively perfume the air, the cookie stands above all in terms of its essence—whatever the feeling of home is, the scent of cookie dough being transformed in an oven is a powerful realization of it. While that's a bold claim, it does have some evidence backing it—some realtors actually bake cookies before holding an open house, knowing that the warm responses the smell will inevitably elicit in potential buyers might well be enough to get them to look past some flaw, or convince themselves that this particular home is destined for them, perhaps encouraging them to enter into—and triumph in—a bidding war.

While smell is the sense that cookies score the highest marks with, taste is not far behind. Simply put, no other category of desserts can succeed with the variety of flavors that the cookie can, moving effortlessly from the sharp sweetness of alfajores to the indulgent, buttery taste of a properly made shortbread to fully savory, finding success and fans with each massive shift.

With smell and taste firmly on their side, we likely already have enough to back up our assertion that cookies have the power to seize the mind like no other dessert. But they also enjoy a unique relationship to texture. For most foods that qualify as treats, the most desirable texture is clear, and incredibly dangerous to depart from—you want potato chips to be crispy, caramels to be chewy, pastries to be airy. But this is not the case with cookies, which have no overarching ideal. Certain cookies want to be chewy, others crumbly.

Some people like their cookies just-cooked and gooey, while others want them to be cracker-crisp. This ability to find success in a number of different forms and feels is another large part of cookies' tremendous appeal, as they have something to satisfy every preference, soothe every tangible craving.

As though these tremendous advantages weren't enough, cookies enjoy another massive leg up in the sweets world—it is easy to indulge while remaining sensible. No matter how outsized the sweet tooth, indulging it is, for the most part, a double-edged sword. The act of consumption is, of course, delightful, but the aftermath is rarely as pleasant, as your body reckons with the rush of fats and sugar, desperately searching for something wholesome to turn into energy. For instance, a piece of cake is a glorious thing, but to partake in one in the middle of the day is difficult if one does not have a fully clear schedule, as the couch will almost certainly soon be calling. That potential for disaster does not exist with cookies, as just one following a meal, or beside a cup of coffee or tea is more than enough to assuage a sweet craving, but nowhere near enough to lay waste to your plans for the remainder of the day. At a time where moderation feels increasingly out of reach, the cookie is a perfectly sized treat, always enough to help, never enough to harm.

This ability to succeed while promoting small servings is closely tied to another reason that cookies seem to aim straight for the heart—altruism is baked into their very essence. As they will only be at their peak for a few days, one needs to think beyond their own enjoyment to be spurred into getting out their baking supplies and whipping up a batch. Whether it is a friend struggling through a difficult time, a child away at college, or a group of friends and family at a holiday party, someone else is usually the catalyst for cookie making, a selfless warmth that suffuses the end result and provides cookies a unique energy that results in numerous celebrations—such as this book.

ESSENTIAL TIPS & TECHNIQUES

As baking well is based on one's ability to master the fundamentals, it's important to take a moment and go in depth into everything from measuring and mixing to working with your home oven. Small things make a big difference in the kitchen, and often determine whether the result is a success or a disappointment. A number of factors can influence the final outcome, but when something really goes wrong, it is almost certain that you got a little bit cocky and glossed over something here.

To start, always read the recipe before you begin to bake. Once you read it, read it again. One of the most common and detrimental mistakes in cooking is starting a preparation without reading the recipe all the way through, and making the necessary, well, preparations. Take the time to go through the recipe so you can see how much time you will need, what ingredients are required, what items need to be at room temperature, etc. Reading the recipe carefully allows you to get organized, so that you can focus on executing when the time comes. It's easy to leave something out or miss a key step when you're rushing to grab items and containers as you go. This rushing also makes it much harder to pay attention to how a certain batter feels while mixing it, hindering the sixth sense that is essential for overcoming the inevitable changes in conditions and ingredients.

After reading the recipe, do yourself a huge favor and set up your kitchen before you plan to bake. Get out your utensils, get your pans ready, and scale your ingredients. This latter activity will make mixing much easier, since measuring and mixing faultlessly at the same time does take a lot of practice. Proper measuring is the most important piece of a finished baked good—make sure you are not rushing or stressed during this part of the process. If you have everything set up beforehand, you can take your time, focus, and pay attention to what is taking place.

Also, make sure your equipment is clean before you start mixing. As in spotless. Any residual fat or grease left on a mixing bowl, mixer attachments, whisk, or spatula can keep the ingredients from incorporating air during the early stages of the mixing process.

Learn to use metric measurements when baking, as it will save you time, prevent waste, and result in fewer dishes, since you can just add everything to the same mixing bowl. This book offers both volume and metric measurements, but we believe that you will have much better results if you commit to using the latter. There is some debate out there on how much 1 cup of a certain ingredient weighs—this book uses the metric equivalents from King Arthur Baking as a reference, since they have an unimpeachable reputation when it comes to baking.

When you talk making cookies, you're usually talking about one crucial step: creaming the butter and sugar together so that these very different ingredients can emulsify and incorporate air into the mixture. To do this, you almost always want to make sure that you are starting the mixing process with softened butter (almost all of the recipes in this book will call

for softened butter, but there are some cookies, like those in the shortbread family, that do better with chilled or cold butter) that is at room temperature. To properly combine butter and sugar, place the softened butter and sugar in the work bowl of a stand mixer fitted with the paddle attachment (you can also use a hand mixer or a sturdy spatula) and beat until the mixture is light and fluffy. This should take 2 to 3 minutes, so do not try to rush this part of the process.

Once the butter and sugar have been creamed, the eggs are often added one at a time, beating well after each addition. This patient incorporating of the eggs ensures that they are fully incorporated.

After the butter, sugar, and eggs have been combined, the recipe typically calls for incorporating the dry ingredients such as flour, baking powder, salt, etc. Make sure to scrape down the work bowl between these additions to prevent clumping and ensure the ingredients are evenly distributed. At all costs, avoid overmixing once the dry ingredients are added, as it can lead to an overly dense texture in the final product. To prevent overmixing, consider placing your dry ingredients on a piece of parchment paper, folding the paper, and gradually adding the ingredients to the work bowl of the stand mixer. Gaining more control over the rate at which products get added to the work bowl promotes even distribution.

Once the cookie dough has been mixed, you need to place the dough on sheet pans and get them in

the oven. When placing cookies on pans, the thing that you want most of all is consistent size—after all, you don't want to mix a dough where everything is perfectly distributed and then undo all that work with a few carelessly formed cookies. Mistakes are easy to avoid with cut-out cookies, since you will be using similar implements to form them. But for drop cookies, press cookies, and cookies that you form into balls, it pays to weigh each cookie using the scale to make sure that each is similarly sized, as this will result in batches that cook evenly.

Once you've got the cookies on the pan, it's time to get them into the oven. And just as every baker is different, every oven is different. If your oven is less than five years old, it is likely to be hotter inside than the temperature you preheated it to. If it is older than five years, your oven may have trouble coming up to and retaining certain temperatures. We highly suggest buying an oven thermometer that you can attach to one of the racks inside your oven, as it will help you better understand your oven and find your ideal temperature for baking cookies.

Once you've successfully navigated all of these steps, your work is all done. Well, almost. Now it's time to let your senses take over and focus on how this particular batch of cookies responds to the heat of the oven. When you see and smell that they are ready, carefully remove them and resist the temptation to pop them directly into your mouth—letting them cool as directed to provide the ideal texture for your cookies.

INGREDIENTS

EGGS

For the purpose of making glorious cookies, it is best to secure the highest-quality eggs available.

It is important to use eggs that have a vibrant orange yolk, as it is a sign of a healthy, happy, and well-fed chicken. Egg yolks get their color from carotenoids, which are also responsible for strengthening the chicken's immune system. Because chickens only hatch eggs if they have sufficient levels of carotenoids, the yolks possess hues of dark gold and orange. Paler yolks are often a result of chickens feeding on barley or white cornmeal, which don't provide as much nourishment as a diet based on yellow corn and marigold petals.

Using brown or white eggs is up to personal preference, since they have the same nutritional profiles and taste. However, there are good arguments for buying brown eggs. Brown eggs come from larger breeds that eat more, take longer to produce their eggs, and produce eggs with thicker protective shells, which prevents internal moisture loss over time and helps eggs maintain their freshness.

Eggs in the United States are graded according to the thickness of their shell and the firmness of their white. Large egg producers can assess the quality of each individual egg and efficiently sort the eggs by size, weight, and quality.

With almost scientific precision, eggs are graded AA (top quality), A (good quality, found in most supermarkets), and B (substandard eggs with thin shells and watery whites that don't reach consumers but are used commercially and industrially). They are also further categorized by size: medium, large, and extra large. In this book, large eggs are what you'll want to use.

The past decade or so has seen a rise in the popularity of free-range and organic eggs. The chickens that produce these eggs are fed organic feed and are caged with slightly more space at their disposal than those raised at conventional chicken farms. The jury is still out on whether free-range eggs taste better, but they constitute an additional, and perhaps politically oriented, option for aspiring bakers.

Also, certain preparations in this book will call for room-temperature eggs. If you're running behind and forgot to set your eggs out and let them come to room temperature, don't worry—just place them in a baking dish or bowl, cover them with warm water, and let them sit for 10 minutes.

DAIRY

In this book, many recipes call for unsalted butter. Salted butter is not the preferred choice because the salt content in each stick of butter varies, making it hard to exercise the necessary control over the amount of salt in your desserts.

Some of you may be wondering: *What about cultured butter?* Though widely available in Europe, cultured butter is something of a specialty item in the United States. With its higher percentage of butterfat, it is essential for light but rich pastries like croissants, but probably not ideal for using to make cookies, as it will lead to unwanted spreading in the oven.

Milk is called for on occasion in the following pages. When it is, without fail, whole milk is what you'll want to use.

SWEETENERS

At least one of the standard sugars—granulated sugar (which is simply called "sugar" in the recipes in this book), confectioners' sugar (which is the same as powdered sugar), and brown sugar (light is what is recommended in this book)—will be required in almost every recipe in this book. But in your endeavors you may come across a recipe that calls for caster sugar, which is a superfine sugar with a consistency that sits somewhere between granulated sugar and confectioners' sugar. Since it can dissolve without heat, unlike granulated sugar, it is most commonly called for in recipes where the sugar needs to melt or dissolve quickly, as in meringues.

As for substituting other sugars in a cookie dough, like demerara and turbinado, keep in mind that they contain more moisture than granulated sugar. This probably won't be a problem in preparations featuring a moist batter, such as brownies. But most cookie recipes are on the arid side, so substituting alternatives might take you wide of the mark.

In certain recipes, a bit of additional sugar is sprinkled on top of the cookies before they are placed in the oven. In these instances, consider using sanding sugar—due to the larger size of its grains, sanding sugar will not fully melt in the oven, giving your cookies a shiny and slightly crusty topping.

Corn syrup is another sweetener called for in a few of the recipes that follow—we recommend using light rather than dark corn syrup, as the latter will have a sizable impact on the final flavor.

FLOUR

The majority of the recipes inside call for all-purpose flour, a versatile white flour that can be relied upon to produce outstanding results in nearly every baking preparation. It is generally a combination of flour from hard wheat (bronze-colored wheat that has a higher protein, and thus higher gluten content) and soft wheat (wheat with a light golden color; also referred to as "white wheat").

Almond flour, hazelnut flour, rice flour, gluten-free flour, and amaranth flour also make appearances in the following recipes. In the preparations where they do appear, expect differences in terms of taste—from nutty to earthy—texture, and color compared to cookies made with all-purpose flour.

CHOCOLATE

Whether it be milk, dark, semisweet, bittersweet, or white, the array of flavors that chocolate provides, and the number of cookies these flavors can carry, leads to its appearance in a number of the recipes in this book.

The rare ingredient that is as comfortable playing with others as it is standing on its own, it's quite possible that chocolate is responsible for putting more

smiles on people's faces than any other ingredient in the world.

In order to produce chocolate, the seeds of the cacao tree are harvested, heaped into piles to ferment, dried in the sun, and roasted at low temperatures to develop the beguiling, beloved flavors. The shells of the beans are then removed, and the resulting nibs are ground into cocoa mass (which is also called "chocolate liquor") and placed under extremely high pressure to produce cocoa powder and cocoa butter. From there, the cocoa powder and cocoa butter are partnered with sugar to produce dark, bittersweet, and semisweet chocolate, and sugar and milk powder to produce milk chocolate.

Dark chocolate has a minimum of 55 percent cocoa and can go all the way to 100 percent, which is extremely bitter, though it carries a highly complex flavor. The dark chocolate you'll use in your cookies will tend to land in the 55 to 65 percent range.

Milk chocolate usually ranges from 38 to 42 percent cocoa and contains milk or heavy cream, along with cocoa beans and sugar. The lower cocoa content creates a creamier and silkier chocolate that is preferred by many.

Now for the question that continues to burn in the minds of many: Is white chocolate *chocolate*? It depends. It does not contain the cocoa mass that is produced by grinding the roasted nibs of the cacao bean finely, so some do not consider white chocolate to be a true chocolate. Some apocryphal tales assert that white chocolate is the result of cocoa beans that have not been roasted; that is far from the case. White chocolate is instead made with cocoa butter (a product resulting from roasted cocoa beans), sugar, and milk powder. One thing white chocolate fans do need to keep in mind when making cookies—white chocolate chips do not melt as well as milk, semisweet, or bittersweet chocolate chips.

VANILLA

While it is synonymous with the bland and flavorless, vanilla is anything but boring. Equal parts smooth and sweet, vanilla has an unmatched ability to both soothe and dazzle the taste buds. Any skeptics out there should talk to their favorite baker about the crucial role vanilla plays in a number of recipes, adding a luscious aroma and lightness whose absence would be glaring, rendering the finished confection unacceptable to anyone who had experienced it previously.

Vanilla is typically categorized according to where the orchid that produces the bean is grown, and, as those who are devotees of the vanilla bean know, there is plenty of variation in its flavor across the globe. Madagascar Bourbon vanilla has nothing to do with American whiskey—though, to be fair, it's an understandable mistake given that many bourbons do carry strong notes of vanilla. Instead, it refers to Bourbon Island (now known as Réunion), an island east of Madagascar in the Indian Ocean, after which the vanilla that grows in the region was named. The sweet, creamy flavor of these beans is what comes to mind when most think of vanilla. Mexican vanilla adds a bit of nutmeg-y spice to vanilla's famously sweet and creamy quality, which makes it a wonderful addition to those cinnamon- and nutmeg-heavy cookies that show up around the holidays (and it can also be used to dress up a barbecue sauce). Indonesian vanilla beans carry a smoky, woody flavor and aroma that are particularly welcome in chocolate-centered cookies. Tahitian vanilla possesses a floral flavor that carries hints of stone fruit and anise, making it a perfect match for cookies containing fruit. Please note that this appellation tendency does not apply to French vanilla. Instead, this name refers to the traditional French method for making ice cream, which utilizes a rich egg custard base. The presence of eggs, some claim, gives vanilla a richness and depth that the bean can't attain on its own, forming such a memorable match that the flavor, which carries caramel and floral notes, resides in a category all its own.

Almost without exception, the recipes in this book recommend pure vanilla extract as opposed to the seeds of a vanilla bean. It is the more common recommendation due to its lower price and the ease of selling larger amounts. While using vanilla bean in place of extract won't do much to the taste, those dark little flecks do add an aesthetic element that the extract cannot, giving any dessert that utilizes the seeds an air of sophistication. If you want to take advantage of this in any recipe that recommends vanilla extract, simply substitute the seeds of a 2-inch piece of vanilla bean for every teaspoon of vanilla extract.

LEAVENING AGENTS

While cookies featuring yeast in the dough do exist, in this book baking powder and baking soda are the two most common leavening agents called for. Baking powder is a mixture of baking soda and cornstarch that enables a baker to go without the acidic components needed to activate regular baking soda to react and leaven. The first reaction occurs when a liquid reacts with the baking soda. The second occurs when heat is added to the equation. Baking soda, or sodium bicarbonate, reacts when combined with acid and heat. Common acidic ingredients in baking are buttermilk, brown sugar, cocoa powder, any citrus juice, vinegar, cream of tartar, sour cream, and yogurt.

DROP EVERYTHING

While drop cookies are downright laissez-faire in the typical hands-on world of baking, they still do require attention. As you'll see when you start working through the recipes in this chapter, we recommend that you weigh each and every portion you drop on the sheet. This small bit of attention will ensure that each batch bakes evenly, resulting in cookies that look positively perfect on the serving tray, with the flavor to match.

YIELD: 16 Cookies
ACTIVE TIME: 15 Minutes
TOTAL TIME: 45 Minutes

BROWN BUTTER CHOCOLATE CHIP COOKIES

By far the king of all cookies. We prefer ours slightly undercooked and just a touch gooey, and we're convinced that this recipe will win you over to our side.

14 tablespoons (197 g) unsalted butter

½ cup (100 g) sugar

¾ cup (150 g) light brown sugar

1 teaspoon (5 g) table salt

2 teaspoons (10 ml) pure vanilla extract

1 (50 g) egg

1 (15 g) egg yolk

2 cups plus 1½ tablespoons (250 g) all-purpose flour

½ teaspoon (2 g) baking soda

1¼ cups (210 g) semisweet chocolate chips

---

1. Preheat the oven to 350°F and line two sheet pans with parchment paper. Place the butter in a saucepan and warm it over medium-high heat until it is starting to brown and give off a nutty aroma (let your nose guide you here, making sure you frequently waft the steam toward you). Transfer the browned butter to the work bowl of a stand mixer fitted with the paddle attachment and let it cool.

2. Add the sugar, brown sugar, salt, and vanilla to the work bowl and cream the mixture on medium speed until it is very light and fluffy, 2 to 3 minutes, scraping down the work bowl as necessary. Add the egg and egg yolk and beat until incorporated, again scraping the work bowl as necessary. Add the flour and baking soda and beat until the mixture comes together as a smooth dough. Add the chocolate chips and beat until they are evenly distributed. Let the dough rest for 5 to 10 minutes.

3. Using a cookie scoop, drop 1 to 1½ oz. (30 to 45 g) portions of the dough on the pans, making sure to leave about 2 inches between each cookie. Place one pan of cookies in the oven at a time. Bake until they are golden brown, 12 to 14 minutes, rotating the pans halfway through.

4. Remove the cookies from the oven, transfer them to a wire rack, and let them cool completely before enjoying.

YIELD: 24 Cookies

ACTIVE TIME: 30 Minutes

TOTAL TIME: 2 Hours

13 tablespoons (184 g) unsalted butter, softened

2½ cups plus 1 tablespoon (510 g) sugar

½ (heaping) cup (185 ml) molasses

2 (100 g) eggs

1½ tablespoons (22.5 ml) white vinegar

5⅓ cups plus 2 tablespoons (650 g) all-purpose flour

2 teaspoons (8 g) baking soda

2 teaspoons (4 g) ground ginger

1 teaspoon (3 g) cinnamon

½ teaspoon (1 g) freshly grated nutmeg

½ teaspoon (3 g) table salt

CHEWY GINGER COOKIES

These rich and chewy cookies are a great, grown-up spin on the gingerbread men we know and love.

---

1. Preheat the oven to 350°F and line three sheet pans with parchment paper. In the work bowl of a stand mixer fitted with the paddle attachment, cream the butter, sugar, and molasses on medium speed until the mixture is very light and fluffy, 2 to 3 minutes, scraping down the work bowl as necessary.
2. Add the eggs one at a time and beat until incorporated, again scraping the work bowl as necessary. When the eggs have been incorporated, scrape down the work bowl, add the vinegar, and beat for another minute. Add the flour, baking soda, ginger, cinnamon, nutmeg, and salt and beat until the mixture comes together as a smooth dough. Let the dough rest for 5 to 10 minutes.
3. Using a cookie scoop, drop 2 oz. (60 g) portions of the dough on the pans, making sure to leave about 3 inches between each cookie. Place one pan of cookies in the oven at a time. Bake, rotating the pans halfway through, until the edges of the cookies are just set, 10 to 12 minutes, taking care not to let them become too crispy.
4. Remove the cookies from the oven, transfer them to a wire rack, and let them cool before enjoying.

YIELD: 24 Cookies
ACTIVE TIME: 30 Minutes
TOTAL TIME: 1 Hour

MEYER LEMON CRINKLE COOKIES

A perfect cookie for springtime, as Meyer lemons add a floral touch to an already light and sweet treat.

1 cup (227 g) unsalted butter, softened

2¼ cups (445 g) sugar

Zest and juice of 2 Meyer lemons

2 (100 g) eggs

2 to 3 drops lemon yellow gel food coloring

3 cups (360 g) all-purpose flour

½ teaspoon (2.5 g) baking powder

¼ teaspoon (2 g) baking soda

½ teaspoon (3 g) table salt

2 cups (227 g) confectioners' sugar

---

1. Preheat the oven to 350°F and line two sheet pans with parchment paper. In the work bowl of a stand mixer fitted with the paddle attachment, cream the butter, sugar, and lemon zest on medium speed until the mixture is very light and fluffy, 2 to 3 minutes, scraping down the work bowl as necessary.
2. Add the eggs one at a time and beat until incorporated, again scraping the work bowl as necessary. When the eggs have been incorporated, scrape down the work bowl, add the lemon juice and food coloring, and beat for another minute. Add the flour, baking powder, baking soda, and salt and beat until the mixture comes together as a smooth dough. Let the dough rest for 5 to 10 minutes.
3. Using a cookie scoop, drop 1 to 1½ oz. (30 to 45 g) portions of the dough on the pans. Place the confectioners' sugar in a mixing bowl, toss the cookie dough balls in the sugar until completely coated, and then place them back on the sheet pans, making sure to leave about 2 inches between each cookie.
4. Place one pan of cookies in the oven at a time. Bake until their surfaces are cracked and a cake tester inserted into their centers comes out clean, 12 to 14 minutes, rotating the pans halfway through.
5. Remove the cookies from the oven, transfer them to a wire rack, and let them cool for 20 to 30 minutes before enjoying.

YIELD: 24 Cookies
ACTIVE TIME: 30 Minutes
TOTAL TIME: 2 Hours

½ cup (113 g) unsalted butter, softened

½ cup (135 g) creamy peanut butter

1 cup plus 2 tablespoons (222 g) sugar

1 cup plus 2 tablespoons (240 g) light brown sugar

2 (100 g) eggs

1½ teaspoons (7 ml) pure vanilla extract

3 cups (360 g) all-purpose flour

1 teaspoon (4 g) baking soda

1½ teaspoons (9 g) table salt

2½ cups (425 g) semisweet chocolate chips

PEANUT BUTTER & CHOCOLATE CHIP COOKIES

As everyone knows, no combination in the world of sweets can compete with peanut butter and chocolate.

---

1. Preheat the oven to 350°F and line two sheet pans with parchment paper. In the work bowl of a stand mixer fitted with the paddle attachment, cream the butter, peanut butter, sugar, and brown sugar on medium speed until the mixture is very light and fluffy, 2 to 3 minutes, scraping down the work bowl as necessary.
2. Add the eggs one at a time and beat until incorporated, again scraping the work bowl as necessary. When the eggs have been incorporated, scrape down the work bowl, add the vanilla extract, and beat for another minute. Add the flour, baking soda, and salt and beat until the mixture comes together as a smooth dough. Add the chocolate chips and beat until they are evenly distributed. Let the dough rest for 5 to 10 minutes.
3. Using a cookie scoop, drop 1 to 1½ oz. (30 to 45 g) portions of the dough on the pans, making sure to leave about 2 inches between each cookie. Place one pan of cookies in the oven at a time. Bake, rotating the pans halfway through, until the edges of the cookies are a light golden brown, 10 to 12 minutes, taking care not to let them become too crispy.
4. Remove the cookies from the oven, transfer them to a wire rack, and let them cool before enjoying.

1¼ cups (175 g) hazelnuts, toasted

1 cup (145 g) unsalted almonds, toasted

¾ cup (150 g) sugar

1½ teaspoons (4 g) cinnamon

½ teaspoon (1 g) ground cardamom

½ teaspoon (1 g) freshly grated nutmeg

Zest of 3 oranges

Zest of 2 lemons

1½ cups (180 g) all-purpose flour

2 tablespoons (12 g) unsweetened cocoa powder

½ teaspoon (3 g) table salt

6 tablespoons (85 g) unsalted butter, softened

¾ cup (160 g) light brown sugar

4 (200 g) eggs

1 teaspoon (5 ml) pure vanilla extract

1 cup semisweet chocolate chips (optional)

Vanilla Glaze (optional; see page 351)

YIELD: 30 Cookies
ACTIVE TIME: 20 Minutes
TOTAL TIME: 1 Hour

LEBKUCHEN

Nutty, spicy, and chocolatey, lebkuchen are traditionally enjoyed around the holiday season in Germany.

---

1. Preheat the oven to 350°F and line three sheet pans with parchment paper. Place the hazelnuts, almonds, sugar, cinnamon, cardamom, and nutmeg in a food processor and blitz until the mixture is finely ground and well combined. Add the orange zest and lemon zest and pulse to incorporate. Set the mixture aside.
2. Place the flour, cocoa powder, and salt in a small bowl and whisk to combine. Place the butter and brown sugar in the work bowl of a stand mixer fitted with the paddle attachment and cream until pale and fluffy, scraping down the work bowl as needed. Add the eggs and vanilla, reduce the speed to low, and beat to incorporate.
3. With the mixer running on low, gradually add the flour mixture to the wet mixture and beat until the resulting mixture comes together as a smooth dough. Add the finely ground mixture and beat until incorporated. Let the dough rest for 5 to 10 minutes.
4. Using a cookie scoop, drop 1 to 1½ oz. (30 to 45 g) portions of the dough on the pans, making sure to leave about 2 inches between each cookie. Place one pan of lebkuchen in the oven at a time. Bake until their edges are set and the tops start to crack, 12 to 14 minutes, rotating the pans halfway through.
5. Remove the lebkucken from the oven and let them cool on the sheet pans.
6. For chocolate-covered lebkuchen, place the chocolate chips in a microwave-safe bowl and microwave on medium until they are melted and smooth, removing to stir every 15 seconds. Dredge the lebkucken in the melted chocolate until completely coated and let it set before enjoying. For glazed lebkuchen, place the glaze in a bowl. Dredge the tops of the lebkuchen in the glaze until completely coated and let it set before enjoying.

YIELD: 30 Cookies

ACTIVE TIME: 10 Minutes

TOTAL TIME: 45 Minutes

FLORENTINES

These cookies are believed to have considerable pedigree, as it is thought that a chef in King Louis XIV's court created the confection.

¾ cup (150 g) sugar

1 teaspoon (5 ml) pure vanilla extract

7 tablespoons (105 ml) heavy cream

3 tablespoons (43 g) unsalted butter

1½ cups (150 g) slivered almonds

⅓ cup (45 g) candied citrus peels

⅓ cup (45 g) dried cherries or plums, chopped

⅓ cup (50 g) raisins

1¼ cups (210 g) bittersweet chocolate chips

---

1. Preheat the oven to 400°F and line two sheet pans with parchment paper. Place the sugar, vanilla, and cream in a saucepan and bring to a gentle boil. Immediately remove the pan from heat, add the butter, and stir until it melts. Stir in the almonds, candied citrus peels, cherries, and raisins.
2. Drop 2-teaspoon portions of the mixture on the pans, leaving about 1 inch between them. Place one pan in the oven at a time. Bake until the Florentines are golden brown, 5 to 10 minutes, rotating the pans halfway through.
3. Remove the Florentines from the oven and let them cool on the pans for 5 minutes before transferring them to wire racks to cool completely.
4. Fill a saucepan halfway with water and bring to a gentle simmer. Place the chocolate chips in a heatproof bowl, place it over the simmering water, and stir until they have melted. Spread the melted chocolate on the undersides of the Florentines and let the chocolate set before enjoying.

YIELD: 24 Cookies
ACTIVE TIME: 45 Minutes
TOTAL TIME: 2 Hours and 30 Minutes

RED VELVET CRINKLE COOKIES

If you're a red velvet purist, substitute buttermilk for the vinegar.

½ cup (113 g) unsalted butter, softened

½ cup plus 1 tablespoon (113 g) sugar

¾ (scant) cup (140 g) light brown sugar

2 (100 g) eggs

1 teaspoon (10 ml) pure vanilla extract

2 drops of red gel food coloring

1 tablespoon (15 ml) white vinegar

2 cups plus 2 tablespoons (255 g) all-purpose flour

2 tablespoons (12 g) cocoa powder

1½ teaspoons (7 g) baking powder

½ teaspoon (2.5 g) table salt

2 cups (227 g) confectioners' sugar

---

1. Preheat the oven to 350°F and line two sheet pans with parchment paper. In the work bowl of a stand mixer fitted with the paddle attachment, cream the butter, sugar, and brown sugar on medium speed until the mixture is very light and fluffy, 2 to 3 minutes, scraping down the work bowl as necessary.
2. Add the eggs one at a time and beat until incorporated, again scraping the work bowl as necessary. When both eggs have been incorporated, scrape down the work bowl, add the vanilla, food coloring, and vinegar, and beat for another minute. Add the flour, cocoa powder, baking powder, and salt and beat until the mixture comes together as a smooth dough. Let the dough rest for 5 to 10 minutes.
3. Using a cookie scoop, drop 1 to 1½ oz. (30 to 45 g) portions of the dough on the pans. Place the confectioners' sugar in a mixing bowl, toss the cookies in the sugar until completely coated, and then place them back on the pans, making sure to leave about 2 inches between the cookies.
4. Place one pan of cookies in the oven at a time. Bake until their surfaces are cracked and a cake tester inserted into their centers comes out clean, 12 to 14 minutes, rotating the pans halfway through.
5. Remove the cookies from the oven, transfer them to a wire rack, and let them cool completely before enjoying.

YIELD: 36 Cookies

ACTIVE TIME: 15 Minutes

TOTAL TIME: 3 Hours

CRANBERRY, PUMPKIN SEED & CHOCOLATE CHIP COOKIES

Autumn-inclined ingredients collide in these jam-packed cookies.

1 cup (227 g) unsalted butter, softened

1 cup (210 g) light brown sugar

½ cup (100 g) sugar

2 (100 g) eggs, at room temperature

2 teaspoons (10 ml) pure vanilla extract

3 cups plus 2 tablespoons (375 g) all-purpose flour

1 teaspoon (5 g) baking soda

1 teaspoon (5 g) table salt

1½ cups (255 g) chocolate chips

1 cup (100 g) cranberries, chopped

½ cup (60 g) pumpkin seeds

---

1. Preheat the oven to 350°F and line three sheet pans with parchment paper. In the work bowl of a stand mixer fitted with the paddle attachment, cream the butter, brown sugar, and sugar on medium speed until the mixture is very light and fluffy, 2 to 3 minutes, scraping down the work bowl as necessary.

2. Add the eggs one at a time and beat until incorporated, again scraping the work bowl as necessary. When both eggs have been incorporated, scrape down the work bowl, add the vanilla and beat for another minute. Add the flour, baking soda, and salt and beat until the mixture comes together as a smooth dough. Add the chocolate chips, cranberries, and pumpkin seeds and beat until they are evenly distributed. Let the dough rest for 5 to 10 minutes.

3. Using a cookie scoop, drop 1 to 1½ oz. (30 to 45 g) portions of the dough on the pans, making sure to leave about 2 inches between the cookies. Place one pan of cookies in the oven at a time. Bake until they are a light golden brown, 10 to 12 minutes, rotating the pans halfway through.

4. Remove the cookies from the oven, transfer them to a wire rack, and let them cool completely before enjoying.

YIELD: 18 Cookies
ACTIVE TIME: 15 Minutes
TOTAL TIME: 1 Hour

ALMOND CLOUDS

Light, chewy, and easy to make, you'll find that the heavenly hint in the name is not an accident.

¼ cup (30 g) all-purpose flour

½ cup (56 g) confectioners' sugar, plus more for topping

½ cup (100 g) sugar

2 (60 g) egg whites

1 (scant) cup (227 g) unsweetened almond paste

---

1. Preheat the oven to 350°F and line two sheet pans with parchment paper. Place the flour, confectioners' sugar, sugar, egg whites, and almond paste in a large mixing bowl and work the mixture with your hands until it comes together as an extremely sticky dough.
2. Coat a tablespoon with nonstick cooking spray and use it to drop tablespoons of the dough onto the pans, making sure to leave about 1 inch between the cookies. Place one pan of cookies in the oven at a time. Bake until they are golden brown and their surfaces are cracked, 12 to 14 minutes, rotating the pans halfway through.
3. Remove the cookies from the oven, transfer them to a wire rack, and let them cool completely before enjoying.

YIELD: 24 Cookies
ACTIVE TIME: 15 Minutes
TOTAL TIME: 3 Hours and 30 Minutes

BROWN SUGAR CRACKLE-TOP COOKIES

This classic French cookie may have an elaborate preparation, but the taste and texture that result make the work so worth it.

---

1. Cut the 4½ tablespoons of butter into small cubes. Place it in the work bowl of a food processor, add the brown sugar and pinch of salt, and pulse to combine. Add 10 tablespoons of the flour and pulse until the mixture resembles coarse bread crumbs. Add the vanilla and pulse to incorporate.
2. Scrape the dough onto a piece of parchment paper and shape it into a disk. Cover it with another piece of parchment paper and roll the dough to about 1/16 inch thick. Slide the dough, keeping it between the pieces of parchment paper, onto a cutting board. Cut the dough into 1½-inch circles, place them on a piece of parchment paper, and transfer the parchment paper to the freezer.
3. Preheat the oven to 425°F and line two sheet pans with parchment paper. Place the milk, water, remaining butter, the sugar, and remaining salt in a saucepan and bring the mixture to a boil over high heat. Add the remaining flour, reduce the heat to medium-low, and quickly stir the mixture with a wooden spoon. It will come together as a dough and a light crust will form on the bottom of the pan. Stir for another minute or so, until the dough dries out and becomes very smooth.
4. Place the dough in the work bowl of a stand mixer fitted with the paddle attachment and let it sit for 10 minutes. Incorporate the eggs one at a time and then beat the dough until it is thick and glossy.
5. Scoop heaping tablespoons of the dough onto the pans, making sure to leave 2 inches of space between each one. Place one of the frozen rounds of dough on top of each cookie. Place the cookies in the oven and bake them for 20 minutes. Carefully open the oven door to get rid of any steam, rotate the pans, and bake until the cookies are golden brown, firm, and their tops are cracked, another 10 to 15 minutes.
6. Remove the cookies from the oven, transfer them to a wire rack, and let them cool completely before serving.

½ cup plus 4½ tablespoons (177 g) unsalted butter

½ cup (105 g) light brown sugar

½ teaspoon plus 1 pinch (3 g) table salt

1½ cups plus 2 tablespoons (195 g) all-purpose flour

¾ teaspoon (3.5 ml) pure vanilla extract

½ cup (113 g) whole milk

½ cup (113 g) water

1 tablespoon (13 g) sugar

4 (200 g) eggs, at room temperature

1¾ cups (300 g) chopped milk chocolate

½ cup (113 g) unsalted butter

3 (150 g) eggs

1 cup (200 g) sugar

¾ cup (90 g) all-purpose flour

1 teaspoon (4.5 g) baking powder

⅛ teaspoon (0.7 g) table salt

2 to 3 tablespoons (20 g) finely ground hazelnuts

1 cup (227 g) sour cream

1 cup (113 g) confectioners' sugar

½ cup (113 ml) heavy cream

YIELD: 20 Cookies

ACTIVE TIME: 15 Minutes

TOTAL TIME: 1 Hour and 30 Minutes

MILK CHOCOLATE & SOUR CREAM COOKIES

Sweet, creamy, and pleasantly tart, these icebox cookies are a good option if you're craving cookies in the summertime.

---

1. Preheat the oven to 350°F and line two sheet pans with parchment paper. Bring water to a simmer in a small saucepan. Place the chocolate and butter in a heatproof bowl, place the bowl over the simmering water, and stir the mixture until it is melted and well combined. Remove the bowl from heat and set it aside.
2. In the work bowl of a stand mixer fitted with the paddle attachment, beat the eggs and sugar on medium speed until the mixture is creamy, about 3 minutes. Add the melted chocolate mixture and beat to incorporate. Scrape down the work bowl, add the flour, baking powder, salt, and hazelnuts, and beat until the mixture comes together as a smooth dough. Let the dough rest for 5 to 10 minutes.
3. Using a cookie scoop, drop 1 to 1½ oz. (30 to 45 g) portions of the dough on the pans, making sure to leave 2 inches between them. Make a slight indentation in the center of each cookie. Place one pan of cookies in the oven at a time. Bake until they are just firm, 8 to 10 minutes, rotating the pans halfway through.
4. Remove the cookies from the oven and let them cool on the pans for a few minutes before transferring them to a wire rack to cool completely.
5. Place the sour cream and half of the confectioners' sugar in a mixing bowl and beat the mixture until it is thick. Place the heavy cream and remaining confectioners' sugar in a separate bowl and whip the mixture until it is thick and glossy. Fold the whipped cream into the sour cream mixture.
6. Place a little of the cream in the indentation in each cookie, place the cookies in the refrigerator, and let them chill for at least 30 minutes before enjoying.

YIELD: 36 Cookies
ACTIVE TIME: 15 Minutes
TOTAL TIME: 40 Minutes

PIGNOLI

When making pignoli, or really any cookies calling for almond paste, make sure you are using unsweetened almond paste instead of marzipan, as the latter will make the cookies too sweet, and keep them from rising properly.

1¾ cups (450 g) unsweetened almond paste

1½ cups (170 g) confectioners' sugar

2 tablespoons (42 ml) honey

Pinch of cinnamon

Pinch of table salt

2 (60 g) egg whites, at room temperature

Zest of 1 lemon

¾ cup (105 g) pine nuts

---

1. Preheat the oven to 350°F and line two sheet pans with parchment paper. In the work bowl of a stand mixer fitted with the paddle attachment, beat the almond paste until it is thoroughly broken up. Add the confectioners' sugar and beat the mixture on low until well combined.
2. Add the honey, cinnamon, salt, egg whites, and lemon zest, raise the speed to medium, and beat until the mixture is very thick, about 5 minutes, scraping down the work bowl as needed.
3. Drop tablespoons of dough onto the pans, leaving about 1 inch of space between them. Gently pat a few pine nuts into each of the cookies. Place one pan of cookies in the oven at a time. Bake until they are golden brown, 12 to 14 minutes, rotating the pans halfway through.
4. Remove the cookies from the oven and let them cool on the sheet pans before enjoying.

YIELD: 20 Cookies

ACTIVE TIME: 15 Minutes

TOTAL TIME: 1 Hour

CHOCOLATE & CARAMEL COOKIES

The wonderfully chewy character of these cookies is as much from the batter as it is from the caramel.

½ cup (113 g) unsalted butter, softened

¼ cup plus 2 tablespoons (65 g) sugar

¼ cup (53 g) light brown sugar

2 (100 g) eggs

¼ teaspoon (1.2 ml) pure vanilla extract

1⅓ cups (160 g) all-purpose flour

½ teaspoon (2 g) table salt

½ cup (42 g) cocoa powder

½ teaspoon (2 g) baking soda

3½ oz. (100 g) soft caramel candies, chopped

---

1. Preheat the oven to 350°F and line two sheet pans with parchment paper. In the work bowl of a stand mixer fitted with the paddle attachment, cream the butter, sugar, and brown sugar on medium speed until the mixture is very light and fluffy, 2 to 3 minutes, scraping down the work bowl as necessary.

2. Add eggs one at a time and beat until incorporated, again scraping the work bowl as necessary. When the eggs have been incorporated, scrape down the work bowl, add the vanilla and beat to incorporate. Add the flour, salt, cocoa powder, and baking soda and beat until the mixture comes together as a smooth dough. Add the caramels and beat until they are evenly distributed. Let the dough rest for 5 to 10 minutes.

3. Using a cookie scoop, drop 1 to 1½ oz. (30 to 45 g) portions of the dough on the pans, making sure to leave 2 inches between them. Place one pan of cookies in the oven at a time. Bake until they are golden brown and their edges are set, 12 to 14 minutes, rotating the pans halfway through.

4. Remove the cookies from the oven and let them cool on the pans for a few minutes. Transfer the cookies to wire racks and let them cool completely before enjoying.

YIELD: 20 Cookies
ACTIVE TIME: 15 Minutes
TOTAL TIME: 1 Hour

½ cup (113 g) unsalted butter, softened

¾ cup (150 g) sugar

1 (50 g) egg

½ teaspoon (2.5 ml) pure vanilla extract

¼ teaspoon (1 ml) peppermint extract

1⅙ cups (140 g) all-purpose flour, sifted

½ cup (45 g) cocoa powder

½ teaspoon (2 g) baking powder

Peppermint candies, crushed, to top

Chocolate Ganache (see page 351), warm, to top

CHOCOLATE & PEPPERMINT COOKIES

Should you be a bigger fan of chocolate than peppermint, consider dipping these cookies halfway or three-quarters of the way into the ganache, then just dusting the coated segment with crushed peppermint candies.

---

1. Preheat the oven to 350°F and line two sheet pans with parchment paper. In the work bowl of a stand mixer fitted with the paddle attachment, cream the butter and sugar on medium speed until the mixture is very light and fluffy, 2 to 3 minutes, scraping down the work bowl as necessary.
2. Add the egg and beat until incorporated, again scraping the work bowl as necessary. When the egg has been incorporated, add the vanilla and peppermint extract, and beat for another minute. Add the flour, cocoa powder, and baking powder, and beat until the mixture comes together as a smooth dough. Let the dough rest for 5 to 10 minutes.
3. Using a cookie scoop, drop 1 to 1½ oz. (30 to 45 g) portions of the dough on the pans, making sure to leave about 2 inches between each cookie. Place one pan of cookies in the oven at a time. Bake until their edges are just set and the tops start to crackle, 10 to 12 minutes, rotating the pans halfway through.
4. Remove the cookies from the oven and them cool on the pans for a few minutes. Transfer them to a wire rack and let them cool completely. When the cookies are cool, sprinkle crushed peppermint candies over them. Drizzle ganache over the top and let the ganache set before enjoying.

CHOCOLATE & PEPPERMINT COOKIES

page 47

YIELD: 20 Cookies
ACTIVE TIME: 15 Minutes
TOTAL TIME: 1 Hour

COCONUT, OATMEAL & QUINOA COOKIES

These are good any time of day, but are particularly so at the breakfast table beside a cup of coffee lightened with a generous amount of cream.

½ cup (55 g) rolled oats

¼ cup (45 g) quinoa

½ cup (40 g) unsweetened shredded coconut

1 cup (120 g) all-purpose flour

½ cup (100 g) sugar

¼ teaspoon (1.5 g) table salt

½ cup (70 g) almonds, chopped

½ cup (113 g) unsalted butter

1 tablespoon (20 ml) light corn syrup

1 teaspoon (4 g) baking powder

2 tablespoons (30 ml) boiling water

---

1. Preheat the oven to 350°F and line two sheet pans with parchment paper. Place the oats, quinoa, coconut, flour, sugar, salt, and almonds in a heatproof mixing bowl and stir to combine.
2. Place the butter and corn syrup in a small saucepan and warm the mixture over medium heat until the butter has melted. Remove the pan from heat. Stir the baking powder and boiling water together in a measuring glass and then carefully stir the mixture into the melted butter mixture.
3. Make a well in the middle of the dry mixture and pour the butter mixture into the well. Stir gently until the mixture holds together.
4. Drop generous tablespoons of the dough on the pans, making sure to leave about 1 inch between them. Coat the bottom of a measuring cup with nonstick cooking spray and use it to gently press down on each cookie, flattening them slightly. Place one pan of cookies in the oven at a time. Bake until they are set and golden brown, 13 to 15 minutes.
5. Remove the cookies from the oven and let them cool on the pans for a few minutes before transferring to a wire rack to cool completely.

1½ cups (255 g) chopped bittersweet chocolate

9 tablespoons (128 g) unsalted butter, softened

1 cup (200 g) light brown sugar

¾ teaspoon (3.5 ml) pure vanilla extract

2 (100 g) eggs

1⅔ cups (200 g) all-purpose flour

⅘ cup (70 g) cocoa powder

2 teaspoons (8.5 g) baking powder

1 teaspoon (5 g) table salt

2 cups (227 g) confectioners' sugar

YIELD: 20 Cookies

ACTIVE TIME: 45 Minutes

TOTAL TIME: 2 Hours and 30 Minutes

CHOCOLATE CRINKLE COOKIES

Somewhere between a brownie and a cookie, these are an ideal blend of richness and sweetness.

---

1. Preheat the oven to 350°F and line two sheet pans with parchment paper. Bring water to a simmer in a small saucepan. Place the chocolate in a heatproof bowl, place the bowl over the simmering water, and stir the chocolate until it is melted. Remove the bowl from heat and set it aside.
2. In the work bowl of a stand mixer fitted with the paddle attachment, cream the butter, brown sugar, and vanilla on medium speed until the mixture is very light and fluffy, 2 to 3 minutes, scraping down the work bowl as necessary. Reduce the speed to low, add the melted chocolate, and beat until incorporated, scraping down the work bowl as needed.
3. Add the eggs one at a time and beat until incorporated, again scraping the work bowl as necessary. Add the flour, cocoa powder, baking powder, and salt and beat until the mixture comes together as a smooth dough. Let the dough rest for 5 to 10 minutes.
4. Using a cookie scoop, drop 1 to 1½ oz. (30 to 45 g) portions of the dough on the pans. Place the confectioners' sugar in a mixing bowl, toss the cookies in the sugar until completely coated, and then place them back on the pans, making sure to leave about 2 inches between the cookies.
5. Place one pan of cookies in the oven at a time. Bake until their surfaces are cracked and a cake tester inserted into their centers comes out clean, 12 to 14 minutes, rotating the pans halfway through.
6. Remove the cookies from the oven, transfer them to a wire rack, and let them cool completely before enjoying.

YIELD: 24 Cookies
ACTIVE TIME: 15 Minutes
TOTAL TIME: 1 Hour

ANZAC BISCUITS

Australia's favorite cookie achieved this status during a time of hardship, as soldiers' wives in World War I were looking for a treat that could keep while in the mail. Today, the recipe has been tweaked, but the anzac biscuit retains its hardy character.

1 cup (90 g) rolled oats

1 cup (120 g) all-purpose flour, plus more as needed

¾ cup (150 g) sugar

Pinch of table salt

¾ cup (60 g) unsweetened shredded coconut

⅔ cup (90 g) slivered almonds

½ cup (113 g) unsalted butter

2 tablespoons (40 ml) light corn syrup

1½ teaspoons (7 g) baking powder

2½ tablespoons (37.5 ml) boiling water

---

1. Preheat the oven to 350°F, line two sheet pans with parchment paper, and coat them with nonstick cooking spray. Place the oats, flour, sugar, salt, coconut, and almonds in a large mixing bowl and stir to combine. Set the mixture aside.

2. Place the butter and corn syrup in a saucepan and warm over medium heat until the mixture starts to bubble. Place the baking powder and boiling water in a large, heatproof mixing bowl. While stirring, carefully add the butter-and-corn syrup mixture to the bowl and stir until the mixture stops bubbling. Add the dry mixture and stir until the mixture comes together as a smooth dough. Let the dough rest for 5 to 10 minutes.

3. Using a cookie scoop, drop 1 to 1½ oz. (30 to 45 g) portions of the dough on the pans, making sure to leave about 2 inches between the cookies. Place one pan of cookies in the oven at a time. Bake until they are crispy and golden brown, 13 to 15 minutes, rotating the pans halfway through.

4. Remove the cookies from the oven and let them cool on the pans for a few minutes. Transfer them to wire racks and let them cool completely before enjoying.

YIELD: 16 Cookies
ACTIVE TIME: 15 Minutes
TOTAL TIME: 1 Hour

OATMEAL, APRICOT & LAVENDER COOKIES

These cookies are a textural wonder, pulling off the impossible by being simultaneously melt-in-your-mouth and chewy.

½ cup (113 g) unsalted butter, softened

½ cup (113 g) cream cheese, softened

¼ teaspoon (1 ml) pure vanilla extract

½ cup (100 g) sugar

⅔ cup (80 g) all-purpose flour

½ teaspoon (2.5 g) table salt

⅓ cup (45 g) dried apricots, finely diced

½ cup (55 g) rolled oats

1 tablespoon (1.5 g) dried lavender buds

1. Preheat the oven to 350°F and line three sheet pans with parchment paper. In the work bowl of a stand mixer fitted with the paddle attachment, cream the butter, cream cheese, vanilla, and sugar on medium speed until the mixture is very light and fluffy, 2 to 3 minutes, scraping down the work bowl as necessary.

2. Add the flour and salt and beat until the mixture comes together as a smooth dough. Add the apricots, oats, and lavender and beat until they are evenly distributed. Let the dough rest for 5 to 10 minutes.

3. Using a cookie scoop, drop 1 to 1½ oz. (30 to 45 g) portions of the dough on the pans, making sure to leave about 2 inches between the cookies. Place one pan of cookies in the oven at a time. Bake until they are a light golden brown, 10 to 12 minutes, rotating the pans halfway through.

4. Remove the cookies from the oven and let them cool on the pans for a few minutes. Transfer them to wire racks and let them cool completely before enjoying.

YIELD: 18 Cookies
ACTIVE TIME: 15 Minutes
TOTAL TIME: 1 Hour

AUTUMN-SPICED OATMEAL & CRANBERRY COOKIES

A cookie that will pair perfect with a cup of chai or a pumpkin spice latte.

¾ cup (170 g) unsalted butter, softened

¾ cup (160 g) light brown sugar

2 (100 g) eggs

1 teaspoon (5 ml) pure vanilla extract

1½ cups (180 g) all-purpose flour

¾ teaspoon (3.5 g) baking soda

½ teaspoon (1 g) cinnamon

½ teaspoon (1 g) freshly grated nutmeg

¼ teaspoon (0.5 g) pumpkin spice

2 cups (225 g) rolled oats

1 cup (115 g) dried cranberries

---

1. Preheat the oven to 350°F and line two sheet pans with parchment paper. In the work bowl of a stand mixer fitted with the paddle attachment, cream the butter and brown sugar until the mixture is very light and fluffy, 2 to 3 minutes, scraping down the work bowl as necessary.
2. Add the eggs one at a time and beat until incorporated, again scraping the work bowl as necessary. When both eggs have been incorporated, scrape down the work bowl, add the vanilla and beat for another minute. Add the flour, baking soda, cinnamon, nutmeg, and pumpkin spice and beat until the mixture comes together as a smooth dough. Add the oats and cranberries and beat until they are evenly distributed. Let the dough rest for 5 to 10 minutes.
3. Using a cookie scoop, drop 1 to 1½ oz. (30 to 45 g) portions of the dough on the pans, making sure to leave about 2 inches between the cookies. Place one pan of cookies in the oven at a time. Bake until they are a light golden brown, 10 to 12 minutes, rotating the pans halfway through.
4. Remove the cookies from the oven and let them cool on the pans for a few minutes. Transfer the cookies to a wire rack and let them cool completely before enjoying.

YIELD: 24 Cookies
ACTIVE TIME: 15 Minutes
TOTAL TIME: 3 Hours

BLACK & WHITE COOKIES

Standing somewhere between a cake and a cookie, New York City's love for this cookie is so profound it was immortalized on an episode of *Seinfeld.*

---

1. Preheat the oven to 350°F and line three sheet pans with parchment paper. In the work bowl of a stand mixer fitted with the paddle attachment, cream the butter and sugar until the mixture is very light and fluffy, 2 to 3 minutes, scraping down the work bowl as necessary.

2. Add the eggs one at a time and beat until incorporated, again scraping the work bowl as necessary. When both eggs have been incorporated, scrape down the work bowl, add the vanilla and beat for another minute. Add the baking powder and salt and beat to incorporate. With the mixer running, gradually add the flour and milk, alternating between them, until the mixture comes together as a smooth dough. Let the dough rest for 5 to 10 minutes.

3. Using a cookie scoop, drop 2 oz. (60 g) portions of the dough on the pans, making sure to leave about 3 inches between the cookies. Coat the bottom of a measuring cup with nonstick cooking spray and use it to gently press down on each cookie, flattening them slightly.

4. Place one pan of cookies in the oven at a time. Bake until their edges are golden brown, 13 to 15 minutes, rotating the pans halfway through.

5. Remove the cookies from the oven, transfer them to a wire rack, and let them cool completely. When the cookies have cooled, spread the Vanilla Glaze on one half of each cookie. Place the iced cookies on wire racks and let the glaze set for 15 minutes. Spread the Coating Chocolate on the other half of each cookie and let set for 1 hour before enjoying.

- 1 cup (227 g) unsalted butter, softened
- 1½ cups (300 g) sugar
- 2 (100 g) eggs
- 1 teaspoon (5 ml) pure vanilla extract
- ½ teaspoon (2 g) baking powder
- ½ teaspoon (2 g) table salt
- 3½ cups (420 g) all-purpose flour
- 1 cup (227 ml) whole milk
- Vanilla Glaze (see page 351), to top
- Coating Chocolate (see page 352), to top

YIELD: 16 Cookies
ACTIVE TIME: 15 Minutes
TOTAL TIME: 1 Hour

BLUEBERRY BUTTERMILK COOKIES

¼ cup (57 g) unsalted butter, softened

¼ cup (50 g) sugar, plus more to top

1 teaspoon (4.5 g) baking soda

1 teaspoon (2.5 g) cinnamon

1¼ cups (150 g) all-purpose flour

½ cup (113 ml) buttermilk

¾ cup (110 g) blueberries

For a bit more sweetness, consider coating these with some Vanilla Glaze (see page 351), swapping in buttermilk for half, or all, of the milk in the glaze.

---

1. Preheat the oven to 350°F and line two sheet pans with parchment paper. In the work bowl of a stand mixer fitted with the paddle attachment, cream the butter and sugar until the mixture is very light and fluffy, 2 to 3 minutes, scraping down the work bowl as necessary.
2. Add the baking soda and cinnamon and beat to incorporate. With the mixer running, gradually add the flour and buttermilk, alternating between them, until the mixture comes together as a smooth dough. Add the blueberries and beat until they are evenly distributed. Let the dough rest for 5 to 10 minutes.
3. Using a cookie scoop, drop 1 to 1½ oz. (30 to 45 g) portions of the dough on the pans, making sure to leave about 2 inches between the cookies. Sprinkle additional sugar over the cookies. Place one pan of cookies in the oven at a time. Bake until their edges are a light golden brown, 10 to 12 minutes, rotating the pans halfway through.
4. Remove the cookies from the oven, transfer them to a wire rack, and let them cool completely before enjoying.

YIELD: 24 Cookies
ACTIVE TIME: 40 Minutes
TOTAL TIME: 2 Hours

BUTTERSCOTCH, TOFFEE & PECAN COOKIES

Make sure you have a crowd coming through when you plan to make these: the decadent trio of add-ins means that just one cookie will be enough for most.

2 cups (210 g) pecans

1 cup (227 g) unsalted butter, softened

½ cup (100 g) sugar

½ cup (105 g) light brown sugar

2 (100 g) eggs

2¼ cups (270 g) all-purpose flour

½ teaspoon (2 g) baking soda

½ teaspoon (2.5 g) table salt

¾ cup (113 g) toffee bits

1⅔ cups (285 g) butterscotch chips

---

1. Preheat the oven to 350°F and line two sheet pans with parchment paper. Place the pecans on a separate sheet pan, place them in the oven, and toast until they are browned and fragrant, 8 to 10 minutes, stirring halfway through. Remove the toasted pecans from the oven and let them cool.

2. In the work bowl of a stand mixer fitted with the paddle attachment, cream the butter, sugar, and brown sugar until the mixture is very light and fluffy, 2 to 3 minutes, scraping down the work bowl as necessary.

3. Add the eggs one at a time and beat until incorporated, again scraping the work bowl as necessary. When both eggs have been incorporated, scrape down the work bowl, add the flour, baking soda, and salt and beat until the mixture comes together as a smooth dough. Add the toffee and butterscotch chips and beat until they are evenly distributed. Chop the toasted pecans, add them to the dough, and beat until they are evenly distributed. Let the dough rest for 5 to 10 minutes.

4. Using a cookie scoop, drop 1 to 1½ oz. (30 to 45 g) portions of the dough on the pans, making sure to leave about 2 inches between the cookies. Place one pan of cookies in the oven at a time. Bake until they are golden brown, 12 to 14 minutes, rotating the pans halfway through.

5. Remove the cookies from the oven, transfer them to a wire rack, and let them cool completely before enjoying.

YIELD: 24 Cookies
ACTIVE TIME: 30 Minutes
TOTAL TIME: 1 Hour

OATMEAL SCOTCHIES

Every cookie lover understands oatmeal's ability to forge powerful partnerships, and that love for collaboration is on full display here.

1 cup (227 g) unsalted butter, softened

½ cup (100 g) sugar

1 cup (210 g) light brown sugar

2 (100 g) eggs

1 tablespoon (20 ml) honey

2 teaspoons (10 ml) pure vanilla extract

1½ cups (180 g) all-purpose flour

½ teaspoon (1 g) cinnamon

1 teaspoon (4.5 g) baking soda

¾ teaspoon (4 g) table salt

3 cups (340 g) rolled oats

2 cups (340 g) butterscotch chips

---

1. Preheat the oven to 350°F and line two sheet pans with parchment paper. In the work bowl of a stand mixer fitted with the paddle attachment, cream the butter, sugar, and brown sugar on medium speed until the mixture is very light and fluffy, 2 to 3 minutes, scraping down the work bowl as necessary.
2. Add the eggs one at a time and beat until incorporated, again scraping the work bowl as necessary. When the eggs have been incorporated, scrape down the work bowl, add the honey and vanilla, and beat for another minute. Add the flour, cinnamon, baking soda, and salt and beat until the mixture comes together as a smooth dough. Add the oats and butterscotch chips and beat until they are evenly distributed. Let the dough rest for 5 to 10 minutes.
3. Using a cookie scoop, drop 1 to 1½ oz. (30 to 45 g) portions of the dough on the pans, making sure to leave about 2 inches between each cookie. Place one pan of cookies in the oven at a time. Bake until their edges are a light golden brown, 10 to 12 minutes, rotating the pans halfway through.
4. Remove the cookies from the oven, transfer them to a wire rack, and let them cool before enjoying.

OATMEAL SCOTCHIES

page 65

10g Gewürz

YIELD: 24 Cookies
ACTIVE TIME: 15 Minutes
TOTAL TIME: 1 Hour

CARROT CAKE COOKIES

These cookies will have plenty of flavor without the Cream Cheese Frosting, so you may just want to have a jar of it beside them, in case some people heard "carrot cake" and got their hopes up.

- ¾ cup (170 g) unsalted butter, softened
- ½ cup (100 g) sugar
- 1 (50 g) egg
- 1¾ cups (210 g) all-purpose flour
- Pinch of table salt
- 1¼ teaspoons (5.5 g) baking powder
- ½ teaspoon (1 g) cinnamon
- ½ teaspoon (1 g) turmeric
- 1½ cups (185 g) rolled oats
- 2 carrots (120 g), peeled and grated
- ⅓ cup (45 g) golden raisins
- Cream Cheese Frosting (optional; see page 352), to top

---

1. Preheat the oven to 350°F and line two sheet pans with parchment paper. In the work bowl of a stand mixer fitted with the paddle attachment, cream the butter and sugar until the mixture is very light and fluffy, 2 to 3 minutes, scraping down the work bowl as necessary.
2. Add the egg and beat until incorporated. Scrape down the work bowl, add the flour, baking powder, cinnamon, and turmeric and beat until the mixture comes together as a smooth dough. Add the oats, carrots, and raisins and beat until they are evenly distributed. Let the dough rest for 5 to 10 minutes.
3. Using a cookie scoop, drop 1 oz. (30 g) portions of the dough on the pans, making sure to leave about 2 inches between the cookies. Place one pan of cookies in the oven at a time. Bake until they are golden brown, 12 to 14 minutes, rotating the pans halfway through.
4. Remove the cookies from the oven and let them cool on the pans for a few minutes. Transfer the cookies to a wire rack and let them cool completely before spreading the frosting (if desired) over them and enjoying.

YIELD: 24 Cookies
ACTIVE TIME: 15 Minutes
TOTAL TIME: 1 Hour

CHESTNUT & CHOCOLATE CHIP COOKIES

Sweet and buttery, chestnuts are a supremely underrated ingredient in the world of baking.

1 cup (227 g) unsalted butter, softened

1 cup (200 g) sugar

1 cup (213 g) light brown sugar

2 (100 g) eggs

1 teaspoon (5 ml) pure vanilla extract

3 cups (360 g) all-purpose flour

1 teaspoon (4.5 g) baking soda

Pinch of table salt

1¾ cups (300 g) semisweet chocolate chips

1 cup (150 g) chopped roasted chestnuts

---

1. Preheat the oven to 350°F and line two sheet pans with parchment paper. In the work bowl of a stand mixer fitted with the paddle attachment, cream the butter, sugar, and brown sugar until the mixture is very light and fluffy, 2 to 3 minutes, scraping down the work bowl as necessary.
2. Add the eggs one at a time and beat until incorporated, again scraping the work bowl as necessary. When both eggs have been incorporated, scrape down the work bowl, add the vanilla and beat until incorporated, again scraping the work bowl as necessary. Add the flour, baking soda, and salt and beat until the mixture comes together as a smooth dough. Add the chocolate chips and chestnuts and beat until they are evenly distributed. Let the dough rest for 5 to 10 minutes.
3. Using a cookie scoop, drop 1 to 1½ oz. (30 to 45 g) portions of the dough on the pans, making sure to leave about 2 inches between the cookies. Place one pan of cookies in the oven at a time. Bake until they are golden brown, 12 to 14 minutes, rotating the pans halfway through.
4. Remove the cookies from the oven, transfer them to a wire rack, and let them cool completely before enjoying.

YIELD: 24 Cookies
ACTIVE TIME: 15 Minutes
TOTAL TIME: 1 Hour

CHOCOLATE & COCONUT COOKIES

While any kind of chocolate chips will work here, bittersweet chocolate chips will probably provide the best counter for the coconut.

⅓ cup (75 g) unsalted butter, softened

½ cup (100 g) sugar

⅓ cup (70 g) light brown sugar

1 (50 g) egg

1 teaspoon (5 ml) pure vanilla extract

1 cup (120 g) all-purpose flour

1 teaspoon (4.5 g) baking powder

Pinch of table salt

¾ cup (130 g) chocolate chips

⅔ cup (55 g) unsweetened shredded coconut

---

1. Preheat the oven to 350°F and line two sheet pans with parchment paper. In the work bowl of a stand mixer fitted with the paddle attachment, cream the butter, sugar, and brown sugar until the mixture is very light and fluffy, 2 to 3 minutes, scraping down the work bowl as necessary.
2. Add the egg and beat until incorporated, again scraping the work bowl as necessary. When the egg has been incorporated, scrape down the work bowl, add the vanilla and beat until incorporated. Add the flour, baking powder, and salt and beat until the mixture comes together as a smooth dough. Add the chocolate chips and coconut and beat until they are evenly distributed. Let the dough rest for 5 to 10 minutes.
3. Using a cookie scoop, drop 1 to 1½ oz. (30 to 45 g) portions of the dough on the pans, making sure to leave about 2 inches between the cookies. Place one pan of cookies in the oven at a time. Bake until they are golden brown, 12 to 14 minutes, rotating the pans halfway through.
4. Remove the cookies from the oven, transfer them to a wire rack, and let them cool completely before enjoying.

YIELD: 12 Cookies

ACTIVE TIME: 15 Minutes

TOTAL TIME: 1 Hour

⅓ cup (75 g) unsalted butter

3 (100 g) egg whites

¼ cup (50 g) sugar

⅔ cup (80 g) all-purpose flour

1 tablespoon (20 ml) honey

PIROULINES

Also known as "cigarettes russes" due to their shape, these cookies are a good test for your kitchen skills, as they require quick, precise movements once out of the oven.

---

1. Preheat the oven to 350°F, line two sheet pans with parchment paper, and coat them with nonstick cooking spray. Place the butter in a saucepan and melt it over medium heat. Remove the pan from heat and set it aside.
2. Place the egg whites and sugar in the work bowl of a stand mixer fitted with the whisk attachment and whip until the mixture is thick and glossy, 2 to 3 minutes. Add the melted butter, flour, and honey and whisk until the mixture comes together as a smooth batter.
3. Drop teaspoons of the batter onto the pans and use a rubber spatula to spread them into thin circles. Place one pan of cookies in the oven at a time. Bake until they start to turn golden brown at their edges, about 10 minutes.
4. Remove the piroulines from the oven. Working quickly while the cookies are still soft, lift them onto another piece of parchment paper and roll them into tubes, using a wooden dowel if necessary. Transfer the piroulines to a wire rack and let them cool completely before enjoying.

YIELD: 24 Cookies
ACTIVE TIME: 15 Minutes
TOTAL TIME: 1 Hour

DARK CHOCOLATE & PEANUT COOKIES

Maldon sea salt flakes make a great topper for this cookie.

1 cup (170 g) dark chocolate chips

1 cup (227 g) unsalted butter, softened

1 cup (213 g) light brown sugar

½ teaspoon (2.5 ml) pure vanilla extract

1 (50 g) egg

1¼ cups (150 g) all-purpose flour

¾ teaspoon (3.5 g) baking soda

¾ cup (110 g) unsalted roasted peanuts, chopped

Flaky sea salt, to top

---

1. Preheat the oven to 350°F and line two sheet pans with parchment paper. Bring water to a simmer in a small saucepan. Place the chocolate chips in a heatproof bowl, place the bowl over the simmering water, and stir the chocolate chips until they have melted. Remove the bowl from heat and set it aside.

2. In the work bowl of a stand mixer fitted with the paddle attachment, cream the butter, brown sugar, and vanilla on medium speed until the mixture is very light and fluffy, 2 to 3 minutes, scraping down the work bowl as necessary. Reduce the speed to low, add the melted chocolate, and beat until incorporated, scraping down the work bowl as needed.

3. Add the egg and beat until incorporated, again scraping the work bowl as necessary. Add the flour and baking soda and beat until the mixture comes together as a smooth dough. Add the peanuts and beat until they are evenly distributed. Let the dough rest for 5 to 10 minutes.

4. Using a cookie scoop, drop 1 to 1½ oz. (30 to 45 g) portions of the dough on the pans, making sure to leave 2 inches between them. Place one pan of cookies in the oven at a time. Bake until their edges are set, 10 to 12 minutes, rotating the pans halfway through.

5. Remove the cookies from the oven, transfer them to a wire rack, and sprinkle flaky sea salt over them. Let the cookies cool completely before enjoying.

YIELD: 18 Cookies
ACTIVE TIME: 15 Minutes
TOTAL TIME: 1 Hour

CHOCOLATE & RICE BUBBLE COOKIES

A Crunch bar, cleverly translated into cookie form.

½ cup (113 g) unsalted butter, softened

⅔ cup (132 g) sugar

1 (50 g) egg

1 teaspoon (5 ml) pure vanilla extract

1 cup (120 g) all-purpose flour

½ teaspoon (2 g) baking powder

Pinch of table salt

1½ cups (35 g) crispy rice cereal

⅔ cup (115 g) milk chocolate chips

---

1. Preheat the oven to 350°F and line two sheet pans with parchment paper. In the work bowl of a stand mixer fitted with the paddle attachment, cream the butter and sugar on medium speed until the mixture is very light and fluffy, 2 to 3 minutes, scraping down the work bowl as necessary.
2. Add the egg and beat until incorporated, again scraping the work bowl as necessary. Add the vanilla, beat to incorporate, and scrape down the work bowl. Add the flour, baking powder, and salt and beat until the mixture comes together as a smooth dough. Add the cereal and chocolate chips and beat until they are evenly distributed. Let the dough rest for 5 to 10 minutes.
3. Using a cookie scoop, drop 1 to 1½ oz. (30 to 45 g) portions of the dough on the pans, making sure to leave 2 inches between them. Place one pan of cookies in the oven at a time. Bake until their edges are set, 10 to 12 minutes, rotating the pans halfway through.
4. Remove the cookies from the oven, transfer them to a wire rack, and let them cool completely before enjoying.

YIELD: 20 Cookies
ACTIVE TIME: 15 Minutes
TOTAL TIME: 3 Hours

COCONUT & ALMOND MACAROONS

The almonds supply a lovely bit of crunch amidst all that soft chewiness.

¼ cup (25 g) almond flour

4 (130 g) egg whites, at room temperature

1¼ cups (250 g) sugar

1 teaspoon (5 g) table salt

1 tablespoon (20 ml) honey

2½ cups (200 g) shredded sweetened coconut

1 teaspoon (5 ml) pure vanilla extract

¼ cup (30 g) slivered almonds, chopped

---

1. Place all of the ingredients in a saucepan and warm the mixture over medium heat, stirring continually, until it starts to hold together, about 5 to 7 minutes.

2. Using a rubber spatula, scrape the mixture into a heatproof mixing bowl and cover it with plastic wrap. Chill the mixture in the refrigerator for about 2 hours.

3. Preheat the oven to 350°F, line two sheet pans with parchment paper, and coat them with nonstick cooking spray. Coat a tablespoon with nonstick cooking spray and use it to drop tablespoons of the dough onto the pans, making sure to leave about 1 inch between the cookies. Place one pan of cookies in the oven at a time. Bake until they are a light golden brown, 10 to 15 minutes.

4. Remove the cookies from the oven and let them cool on the pans for a few minutes before transferring them to wire racks to cool completely.

page 79

YIELD: 20 Cookies
ACTIVE TIME: 30 Minutes
TOTAL TIME: 7 Hours and 30 Minutes

ELISEN GINGERBREAD

A classic gingerbread recipe from Nuremberg, Germany, that also happens to be gluten-free.

3 (150 g) eggs

1½ cups (285 g) caster (superfine) sugar

Pinch of ground cloves

1 teaspoon (2.5 g) cinnamon

½ teaspoon (2 g) baking powder

Zest of 1 lemon

3 cups (250 g) almond meal

¼ cup (40 g) chopped dried fruit

Chocolate Ganache (see page 351), warmed, to top

---

1. Line two sheet pans with parchment paper. In the work bowl of a stand mixer fitted with the paddle attachment, cream the eggs and sugar on medium speed until the mixture is very light and fluffy, 2 to 3 minutes, scraping down the work bowl as necessary.
2. Add the cloves, cinnamon, baking powder, and lemon zest, beat to incorporate, and scrape down the work bowl. Add the almond meal and beat until the mixture comes together as a smooth dough. Add the dried fruit and beat until it is evenly distributed. Let the dough rest for 5 to 10 minutes.
3. Using a cookie scoop, drop 1 to 1½ oz. (30 to 45 g) portions of the dough on the pans, making sure to leave 2 inches between them. Smooth the tops of the cookies with a rubber spatula and let them sit at room temperature for 6 hours.
4. Preheat the oven to 325°F. Place one pan of cookies in the oven at a time. Bake until they are browned and slightly puffy, about 20 minutes, rotating the pans halfway through.
5. Remove the cookies from the oven, transfer them to wire racks, and let them cool completely. Spoon the ganache over the cookies and let it set before enjoying.

YIELD: 20 Cookies
ACTIVE TIME: 15 Minutes
TOTAL TIME: 1 Hour

FORTUNE COOKIES

With or without fortunes inside, these cookies are certain to bring a smile to everyone's face.

4 (120 g) egg whites

1 teaspoon (5 ml) pure almond extract

1 teaspoon (5 ml) pure vanilla extract

6 tablespoons (84 g) canola oil

1 cup (120 g) all-purpose flour

1 tablespoon (7 g) cornstarch

½ teaspoon (2 g) table salt

1 cup (200 g) sugar

2 tablespoons (30 ml) water

---

1. Preheat the oven to 300°F, line three sheet pans with parchment paper, and coat them with nonstick cooking spray.
2. Place the egg whites, almond extract, vanilla, and canola oil in the work bowl of a stand mixer fitted with the paddle attachment and beat the mixture until it is frothy. Combine the flour, cornstarch, salt, and sugar in a separate bowl and stir in the water. With the mixer running, gradually add the dry mixture to the work bowl and beat until the resulting mixture comes together as a smooth batter that drops easily off a wooden spoon.
3. Drop tablespoons of the batter on the pans, making sure to leave 3 inches of space between each one. Gently tilt the pans back and forth and from side to side until each tablespoon of batter is a 4-inch circle.
4. Place one pan of cookies in the oven at a time. Bake until their edges are golden brown, 12 to 14 minutes, rotating the pans halfway through. While the cookies are baking, put on thin cotton gloves.
5. Remove the cookies from the oven and, working quickly, use a spatula to turn the warm cookies into your hands. Fold them in half, place them over a wooden spoon, and gently pull the edges downward. Transfer the cookies to a wire rack and let them cool completely before enjoying.

YIELD: 18 Cookies
ACTIVE TIME: 15 Minutes
TOTAL TIME: 1 Hour

GIANDUJA & WALNUT COOKIES

Chocolate enriched by sugar and hazelnuts, gianduja has a luxurious character capable of making even the most straightforward cookies feel like a special occasion.

½ cup (113 g) unsalted butter, softened

1 cup (200 g) sugar

3 (150 g) eggs

1 cup (120 g) all-purpose flour

1 teaspoon (4.5 g) baking powder

Pinch of table salt

½ cup (60 g) minced walnuts

⅔ cup (120 g) gianduja chocolate pieces

---

1. Preheat the oven to 350°F and line two sheet pans with parchment paper. In the work bowl of a stand mixer fitted with the paddle attachment, cream the butter and sugar on medium speed until the mixture is very light and fluffy, 2 to 3 minutes, scraping down the work bowl as necessary.

2. Add the eggs one at a time and beat until incorporated, again scraping the work bowl as necessary. When both eggs have been incorporated, scrape down the work bowl, add the flour, baking powder, and salt and beat until the mixture comes together as a smooth dough. Add the walnuts and beat until they are evenly distributed. Let the dough rest for 5 to 10 minutes.

3. Drop scant tablespoons of the dough on the pans, making sure to leave 1½ inches between them. Coat the bottom of a measuring cup with nonstick cooking spray and use it to gently press down on each cookie, flattening them slightly. Place one pan of cookies in the oven at a time. Bake until their edges are just set, about 15 minutes, rotating the pans halfway through.

4. Remove the cookies from the oven, transfer them to wire racks, and let them cool completely. Fill a small saucepan halfway with water and bring to a simmer. Place the gianduja chocolate in a heatproof bowl, place it over the simmering water, and stir until it is melted and smooth. Dip the cookies into the melted gianduja and let it set before enjoying.

YIELD: 18 Cookies

ACTIVE TIME: 30 Minutes

TOTAL TIME: 2 Hours

DOUBLE SHOT COOKIES

Illy's espresso powder, available at stores around the country, is the best choice for these cookies—and all your baking needs.

- 1¼ cups (215 g) chopped bittersweet chocolate
- 2 tablespoons (30 g) unsalted butter, softened
- ½ cup (100 g) sugar
- ¾ teaspoon (3.5 ml) pure vanilla extract
- 2 (100 g) eggs
- ¼ cup plus 2 teaspoons (35 g) all-purpose flour
- ¼ teaspoon (1 g) baking powder
- ¼ teaspoon (1.5 g) table salt
- ¼ cup (20 g) espresso powder
- 1 cup (170 g) semisweet chocolate chunks

---

1. Preheat the oven to 350°F and line two sheet pans with parchment paper. Fill a small saucepan halfway with water and bring to a simmer. Place the bittersweet chocolate and butter in a heatproof bowl, place it over the simmering water, and stir until they have melted and are combined.
2. Transfer the mixture to the work bowl of a stand mixer fitted with the paddle attachment and let it cool. Add the sugar and vanilla and beat to combine. Add the eggs one at a time and beat until incorporated, scraping down the work bowl as necessary. When both eggs have been incorporated, scrape down the work bowl, add the flour, baking powder, salt, and espresso powder and beat until the mixture comes together as a smooth dough. Add the semisweet chocolate and beat until it is evenly distributed. Let the dough rest for 5 to 10 minutes.
3. Using a cookie scoop, drop 1 to 1½ oz. (30 to 45 g) portions of the dough on the pans, making sure to leave 2 inches between them. Place one pan of cookies in the oven at a time. Bake until a cake tester inserted into their centers comes out clean, 12 to 14 minutes, rotating the pans halfway through.
4. Remove the cookies from the oven, transfer them to wire racks, and let them cool completely before enjoying.

YIELD: 18 Cookies
ACTIVE TIME: 15 Minutes
TOTAL TIME: 1 Hour

GLUTEN-FREE DOUBLE CHOCOLATE COOKIES

For those who are crazy about chocolate, and feel just as strongly about avoiding gluten.

1 cup (170 g) bittersweet chocolate chips

½ cup (113 g) unsalted butter, softened

¼ cup (50 g) sugar

½ cup (105 g) light brown sugar

1 (50 g) egg

1 teaspoon (5 ml) pure vanilla extract

1¼ cups (120 g) almond flour

½ cup (45 g) gluten-free cocoa powder

1 teaspoon (4.5 g) gluten-free baking soda

¼ teaspoon (1.5 g) table salt

---

1. Preheat the oven to 350°F and line two sheet pans with parchment paper. Fill a small saucepan halfway with water and bring to a simmer. Place half of the chocolate in a heatproof bowl, place it over the simmering water, and stir until they have melted. Transfer the melted chocolate to the work bowl of a stand mixer fitted with the paddle attachment and let it cool.
2. Add the butter, sugar, and brown sugar to the work bowl and cream the mixture on medium speed until it is very light and fluffy, 2 to 3 minutes. Add the egg and beat until incorporated, scraping down the work bowl as necessary. When the egg has been incorporated, scrape down the work bowl, add the vanilla, and beat to incorporate. Add the almond flour, cocoa powder, baking soda, and salt and beat until the mixture comes together as a smooth dough. Add the remaining chocolate chips and beat until they are evenly distributed. Let the dough rest for 5 to 10 minutes.
3. Using a cookie scoop, drop 1 to 1½ oz. (30 to 45 g) portions of the dough on the pans, making sure to leave 2 inches between them. Place one pan of cookies in the oven at a time. Bake until their edges are set, 10 to 12 minutes, rotating the pans halfway through.
4. Remove the cookies from the oven, transfer them to wire racks, and let them cool completely before enjoying.

YIELD: 40 Cookies
ACTIVE TIME: 15 Minutes
TOTAL TIME: 1 Hour

GLUTEN-FREE LEMON SUGAR COOKIES

Just a little bit of lemon can transform a cookie recipe that everyone is well acquainted with.

½ cup (113 g) unsalted butter, softened

1 cup (200 g) sugar, plus more to top

1 (50 g) egg

1 tablespoon (6 g) lemon zest

½ teaspoon (5 ml) pure vanilla extract

2 tablespoons (30 ml) fresh lemon juice

1¾ cups (273 g) gluten-free all-purpose flour

½ teaspoon (1.5 g) xanthan gum

½ teaspoon (2 g) baking soda

½ teaspoon (2 g) table salt

Confectioners' sugar, to dust

---

1. Preheat the oven to 350°F and line two sheet pans with parchment paper. In the work bowl of a stand mixer fitted with the paddle attachment, cream the butter and sugar on medium speed until the mixture is very light and fluffy, 2 to 3 minutes, scraping down the work bowl as necessary.

2. Add the egg and beat until it is incorporated, again scraping the work bowl as necessary. When the egg has been incorporated, scrape down the work bowl, add the lemon zest, vanilla, and lemon juice, and beat to incorporate. Add the flour, xanthan gum, baking soda, and salt and beat until the mixture comes together as a smooth dough. Let the dough rest for 5 to 10 minutes.

3. Using a cookie scoop, drop 1 to 1½ oz. (30 to 45 g) portions of the dough on the pans, making sure to leave 2 inches between them. Place one pan of cookies in the oven at a time. Bake until they are golden brown and their edges are set, 10 to 12 minutes, rotating the pans halfway through.

4. Remove the cookies from the oven, transfer them to wire racks, and let them cool completely. Dust the cookies with confectioners' sugar before enjoying.

YIELD: 24 Cookies
ACTIVE TIME: 15 Minutes
TOTAL TIME: 1 Hour

GLUTEN-FREE MUESLI COOKIES

Myriad flavors and textures distract one from noticing that these cookies could actually be presented as a wholesome option for dessert.

---

2 (100 g) eggs

¼ cup (57 g) coconut oil, melted

½ cup (136 g) creamy almond butter

½ cup (75 g) coconut sugar

1 teaspoon (5 ml) pure vanilla extract

1¼ cups (140 g) gluten-free rolled oats

⅔ cup (65 g) almond flour

¾ teaspoon (1.5 g) cinnamon

½ teaspoon (2 g) gluten-free baking powder

½ teaspoon (2 g) table salt

½ cup (80 g) raisins

½ cup (70 g) almonds, chopped

½ cup (70 g) sunflower seeds

Chocolate Ganache (see page 351), warm

1. Preheat the oven to 350°F and line two sheet pans with parchment paper. In the work bowl of a stand mixer fitted with the paddle attachment, combine the eggs, coconut oil, almond butter, coconut sugar, and vanilla and beat until the mixture is smooth and creamy, scraping down the work bowl as necessary.
2. Add the oats, flour, cinnamon, baking powder, and salt and beat until the mixture comes together as a smooth dough. Add the raisins, almonds, and sunflower seeds and beat until they are evenly distributed. Let the dough rest for 5 to 10 minutes.
3. Using a cookie scoop, drop 1 to 1½ oz. (30 to 45 g) portions of the dough on the pans, making sure to leave 2 inches between them. Coat the bottom of a measuring cup with nonstick cooking spray and use it to gently press down on each cookie, flattening them slightly. Place one pan of cookies in the oven at a time. Bake until they are golden brown and their edges are set, 10 to 12 minutes, rotating the pans halfway through.
4. Remove the cookies from the oven and let them cool on the pans for a few minutes. Transfer the cookies to wire racks and let them cool completely. Drizzle the ganache over the cookies and let it set before enjoying.

1½ cups (255 g) chopped Mexican chocolate

9 tablespoons (128 g) unsalted butter, softened

1 cup (213 g) light brown sugar

¾ teaspoon (3.5 ml) pure vanilla extract

2 (100 g) eggs

1⅓ cups (160 g) all-purpose flour

¾ cup plus 1 tablespoon (68 g) cocoa powder

2 teaspoons (9 g) baking powder

½ teaspoon (1 g) cinnamon

¼ teaspoon (1 g) ancho chile powder

1 teaspoon (5 g) table salt

2 cups (227 g) confectioners' sugar

YIELD: 20 Cookies

ACTIVE TIME: 30 Minutes

TOTAL TIME: 2 Hours

MEXICAN CHOCOLATE CRINKLE COOKIES

Chocolate from Taza, though it can be on the pricier side of things, is a great option to utilize in these cookies.

---

1. Preheat the oven to 350°F and line two sheet pans with parchment paper. Bring water to a simmer in a small saucepan. Place the chocolate in a heatproof bowl, place the bowl over the simmering water, and stir the chocolate until it is melted. Remove the bowl from heat and set it aside.
2. In the work bowl of a stand mixer fitted with the paddle attachment, cream the butter, brown sugar, and vanilla on medium speed until the mixture is very light and fluffy, 2 to 3 minutes, scraping down the work bowl as necessary. Reduce the speed to low, add the melted chocolate, and beat until incorporated, scraping down the work bowl as needed.
3. Add the eggs one at a time and beat until incorporated, again scraping the work bowl as necessary. Add the flour, cocoa powder, baking powder, chile powder, and salt and beat until the mixture comes together as a smooth dough. Let the dough rest for 5 to 10 minutes.
4. Using a cookie scoop, drop 1 to 1½ oz. (30 to 45 g) portions of the dough on the pans. Place the confectioners' sugar in a mixing bowl, toss the cookies in the sugar until completely coated, and then place them back on the pans, making sure to leave about 2 inches between the cookies.
5. Place one pan of cookies in the oven at a time. Bake until their surfaces are cracked and a cake tester inserted into their centers comes out clean, 12 to 14 minutes, rotating the pans halfway through.
6. Remove the cookies from the oven, transfer them to a wire rack, and let them cool completely before enjoying.

YIELD: 18 Cookies
ACTIVE TIME: 15 Minutes
TOTAL TIME: 1 Hour

OAT & GOJI BERRY COOKIES

Also known as wolfberries, goji berries' sour flavor keys the surprisingly deep flavor of these treats.

2½ cups (285 g) rolled oats

½ cup (100 g) millet

½ cup (57 g) slivered almonds, chopped

⅓ cup (50 g) raisins, chopped

⅓ cup (50 g) goji berries, chopped

1 teaspoon (2 g) orange zest

½ teaspoon (2 g) baking soda

½ teaspoon fine (2 g) table salt

½ teaspoon (1 g) cinnamon

½ cup (113 g) unsalted butter

2 tablespoons (32 g) creamy peanut butter

¾ cup (160 g) light brown sugar

1 (50 g) egg

1 teaspoon (5 ml) pure vanilla extract

1. Preheat the oven to 350°F and line two sheet pans with parchment paper. Place 1½ cups of the oats in a food processor and pulse until they are finely ground. Transfer them to a mixing bowl and stir in the remaining oats, millet, almonds, raisins, goji berries, orange zest, baking soda, salt, and cinnamon.

2. Melt the butter and peanut butter in a saucepan over medium heat, stirring until the mixture is smooth. Remove the pan from heat and stir in the brown sugar. Add the egg, vanilla, and butter mixture to the mixing bowl and stir until the resulting mixture comes together as a dough.

3. Using a cookie scoop, drop 1 to 1½ oz. (30 to 45 g) portions of the dough on the pans, making sure to leave 2 inches between them. Coat the bottom of a measuring cup with nonstick cooking spray and use it to gently press down on each cookie, flattening them slightly. Place one pan of cookies in the oven at a time. Bake until they are golden brown and their edges are set, 12 to 14 minutes, rotating the pans halfway through.

4. Remove the cookies from the oven and let them cool on the pans for a few minutes. Transfer the cookies to wire racks and let them cool completely before enjoying.

YIELD: 24 Cookies

ACTIVE TIME: 15 Minutes

TOTAL TIME: 1 Hour

OATMEAL, CRANBERRY & WHITE CHOCOLATE COOKIES

It may take a bit of effort, but tracking down some unsweetened dried cranberries will take these cookies to the next level, as the added tartness will cut beautifully against the sweetness of the white chocolate.

⅔ cup (150 g) unsalted butter, softened

3 tablespoons (38 g) sugar

½ cup (105 g) light brown sugar

1 tablespoon (20 ml) light corn syrup

1 tablespoon (15 ml) water

1¼ cups (150 g) all-purpose flour

½ teaspoon (2 g) baking soda

Pinch of table salt

¾ cup (85 g) rolled oats

⅔ cup (115 g) chopped white chocolate

⅔ cup (85 g) dried cranberries

---

1. Preheat the oven to 350°F and line two sheet pans with parchment paper. In the work bowl of a stand mixer fitted with the paddle attachment, cream the butter, sugar, and brown sugar on medium speed until the mixture is very light and fluffy, 2 to 3 minutes, scraping down the work bowl as necessary.
2. Add the corn syrup and water, and beat until incorporated, again scraping the work bowl as necessary. Add the flour, baking soda, and salt and beat until the mixture comes together as a smooth dough. Add the oats, white chocolate, and dried cranberries and beat until they are evenly distributed. Let the dough rest for 5 to 10 minutes.
3. Using a cookie scoop, drop 1 to 1½ oz. (30 to 45 g) portions of the dough on the pans, making sure to leave 2 inches between them. Place one pan of cookies in the oven at a time. Bake until they are golden brown and their edges are set, 12 to 14 minutes, rotating the pans halfway through.
4. Remove the cookies from the oven and let them cool on the pans for a few minutes. Transfer the cookies to wire racks and let them cool completely before enjoying.

YIELD: 18 Cookies

ACTIVE TIME: 15 Minutes

TOTAL TIME: 1 Hour

PECAN, PUMPKIN & CHERRY COOKIES

If so moved, feel free to incorporate any of your favored fall baking spices into this dough.

- 1 cup (120 g) all-purpose flour
- ¾ cup (68 g) quick-cooking oats
- 1 tablespoon (7 g) ground flaxseed
- ½ cup (105 g) light brown sugar
- ¼ cup (50 g) sugar
- 1 teaspoon (2.5 g) cinnamon
- ¼ teaspoon (1.5 g) table salt
- ½ teaspoon (2 g) baking soda
- ½ cup (113 g) pumpkin puree
- ¼ cup (57 g) coconut oil, melted
- 1 teaspoon (5 ml) pure vanilla extract
- ½ cup (80 g) dried cherries

---

1. Preheat the oven to 350°F and line two sheet pans with parchment paper. In the work bowl of a stand mixer fitted with the paddle attachment, combine the flour, oats, flaxseed, brown sugar, sugar, cinnamon, salt, and baking soda. Add the pumpkin puree, coconut oil, and vanilla and beat until the mixture comes together as a smooth dough. Add the cherries and beat until they are evenly distributed. Let the dough rest for 5 to 10 minutes.

2. Using a cookie scoop, drop 1 to 1½ oz. (30 to 45 g) portions of the dough on the pans, making sure to leave 2 inches between them. Place one pan of cookies in the oven at a time. Bake until their edges are set, 10 to 12 minutes, rotating the pans halfway through.

3. Remove the cookies from the oven and let them cool on the pans for a few minutes. Transfer the cookies to wire racks and let them cool completely before enjoying.

YIELD: 24 Cookies
ACTIVE TIME: 20 Minutes
TOTAL TIME: 2 Hours

ORANGE & ROSEMARY CRINKLE COOKIE

If you're interested in letting the orange and rosemary elements really shine, forgo the roll through the confectioners' sugar.

9 tablespoons (128 g) unsalted butter, softened

1 cup (200 g) sugar

¾ teaspoon (3.5 ml) pure vanilla extract

2 (100 g) eggs

2 tablespoons (30 ml) fresh orange juice

1 tablespoon (6 g) orange zest

2 cups (240 g) all-purpose flour

2 teaspoons (9 g) baking soda

1 teaspoon (5 g) table salt

2 teaspoons (2 g) finely chopped fresh rosemary

2 cups (227 g) confectioners' sugar

---

1. Preheat the oven to 350°F and line two sheet pans with parchment paper. In the work bowl of a stand mixer fitted with the paddle attachment, cream the butter, sugar, and vanilla on medium speed until the mixture is very light and fluffy, 2 to 3 minutes, scraping down the work bowl as necessary.

2. Add the eggs one at a time and beat until incorporated, again scraping the work bowl as necessary. Add the orange juice and orange zest and beat to incorporate. Add the flour, baking soda, and salt and beat until the mixture comes together as a smooth dough. Add the rosemary and beat until it is evenly distributed. Let the dough rest for 5 to 10 minutes.

3. Using a cookie scoop, drop 1 to 1½ oz. (30 to 45 g) portions of the dough on the pans. Place the confectioners' sugar in a mixing bowl, toss the cookies in the sugar until completely coated, and then place them back on the pans, making sure to leave about 2 inches between the cookies.

4. Place one pan of cookies in the oven at a time. Bake until their surfaces are cracked and a cake tester inserted into their centers comes out clean, 12 to 14 minutes, rotating the pans halfway through.

5. Remove the cookies from the oven, transfer them to a wire rack, and let them cool completely before enjoying.

YIELD: 18 Cookies
ACTIVE TIME: 15 Minutes
TOTAL TIME: 1 Hour

SALTED TOFFEE & CHOCOLATE COOKIES

The hint of salt in the toffee elevates all of the other flavors present in this recipe.

- 1 cup (227 g) unsalted butter, softened
- ½ cup (100 g) sugar
- ⅓ cup (70 g) light brown sugar
- 1 (50 g) egg
- 1¼ cups (150 g) all-purpose flour
- ½ teaspoon (2 g) baking soda
- Pinch of table salt
- 1 cup (170 g) semisweet chocolate chips
- 1 cup (320 ml) Salted Toffee (see page 353)

---

1. Preheat the oven to 350°F and line two sheet pans with parchment paper. In the work bowl of a stand mixer fitted with the paddle attachment, cream the butter, sugar, and brown sugar on medium speed until the mixture is very light and fluffy, 2 to 3 minutes, scraping down the work bowl as necessary.
2. Add the egg and beat until incorporated, again scraping the work bowl as necessary. When the egg has been incorporated, scrape down the work bowl, add the flour, baking soda, and salt and beat until the mixture comes together as a smooth dough. Add the chocolate chips and beat until they are evenly distributed. Reduce the speed to low and add the toffee, swirling it through the dough. Let the dough rest for 5 to 10 minutes.
3. Using a cookie scoop, drop 1 to 1½ oz. (30 to 45 g) portions of the dough on the pans, making sure to leave 2 inches between them. Coat the bottom of a measuring cup with nonstick cooking spray and use it to gently press down on each cookie, flattening them slightly. Place one pan of cookies in the oven at a time. Bake until they are golden brown and their edges are set, 12 to 14 minutes, rotating the pans halfway through.
4. Remove the cookies from the oven and let them cool on the pans for a few minutes. Transfer the cookies to wire racks and let them cool completely before enjoying.

ORANGE & ROSEMARY CRINKLE COOKIE

page 104

YIELD: 24 Cookies

ACTIVE TIME: 15 Minutes

TOTAL TIME: 1 Hour

STRAWBERRY SHORTCAKE COOKIES

If you see the name of these cookies and envision them topped with whipped cream instead of the icing recommended here, we encourage you to indulge that inclination.

2 cups (300 g) fresh strawberries, hulled and finely diced

1 teaspoon (5 ml) fresh lemon juice

½ cup plus 1 tablespoon (113 g) sugar

2 cups (240 g) all-purpose flour

½ teaspoon (3 g) table salt

2 teaspoons (9 g) baking powder

6 tablespoons (85 g) unsalted butter, chilled and chopped

⅔ cup (150 ml) heavy cream

Royal Icing (see page 353), to top

---

1. Preheat the oven to 350°F and line two sheet pans with parchment paper. Combine the strawberries, lemon juice, and 1 tablespoon of sugar in a mixing bowl. In a separate mixing bowl, combine the flour, salt, baking powder, and remaining sugar. Add the butter to the flour mixture and work it with a pastry cutter until the mixture resembles coarse bread crumbs.

2. Stir in the cream and work the mixture until it starts to come together as a soft dough. Add the strawberry mixture and gently stir until it is evenly distributed. Let the dough rest for 5 to 10 minutes.

3. Using a cookie scoop, drop 1 to 1½ oz. (30 to 45 g) portions of the dough on the pans, making sure to leave 2 inches between them. Place one pan of cookies in the oven at a time. Bake until they are golden brown and their edges are set, 12 to 14 minutes, rotating the pans halfway through.

4. Remove the cookies from the oven, transfer them to wire racks, and let them cool completely. Drizzle the icing over the cookies and enjoy.

YIELD: 18 Cookies
ACTIVE TIME: 15 Minutes
TOTAL TIME: 2 Hours

TRAIL MIX COOKIES

Don't hesitate to make these your own, incorporating whatever items you'd want in your trail mix before heading out on a hike.

½ cup (113 g) unsalted butter, softened

¼ cup (50 g) sugar

½ cup (105 g) light brown sugar

1 teaspoon (5 ml) pure vanilla extract

1 (50 g) egg

1⅓ cups (160 g) all-purpose flour

2 tablespoons (14 g) cornstarch

Pinch of table salt

1 cup (113 g) rolled oats

⅔ cup (90 g) sunflower seeds

1 cup (150 g) raisins

1. Preheat the oven to 350°F and line two sheet pans with parchment paper. In the work bowl of a stand mixer fitted with the paddle attachment, cream the butter, sugar, and brown sugar on medium speed until the mixture is very light and fluffy, 2 to 3 minutes, scraping down the work bowl as necessary.
2. Add the egg and beat until incorporated, again scraping the work bowl as necessary. When the egg has been incorporated, scrape down the work bowl, add the flour, cornstarch, and salt, and beat until the mixture comes together as a smooth dough. Add the oats, sunflower seeds, and raisins and beat until they are evenly distributed. Let the dough rest for 5 to 10 minutes.
3. Using a cookie scoop, drop 1 oz. (30 g) portions of the dough on the pans, making sure to leave 2 inches between them. Place one pan of cookies in the oven at a time. Bake until they are golden brown and dry to the touch, 13 to 15 minutes, rotating the pans halfway through.
4. Remove the cookies from the oven and let them cool on the pans for a few minutes. Transfer the cookies to wire racks and let them cool completely before enjoying.

YIELD: 24 Cookies

ACTIVE TIME: 15 Minutes

TOTAL TIME: 2 Hours

TRIPLE CHOCOLATE COOKIES

Because some of us can't ever get enough chocolate.

1¼ cups (210 g) bittersweet chocolate chunks

⅓ cup (75 g) unsalted butter, softened

1 teaspoon (5 ml) pure vanilla extract

¾ cup (160 g) light brown sugar

1¼ cups (140 g) self-rising flour

1 tablespoon (5 g) cocoa powder

½ teaspoon (2 g) table salt

⅔ cup (110 g) milk chocolate chunks

---

1. Preheat the oven to 350°F and line two sheet pans with parchment paper. Fill a small saucepan halfway with water and bring it to a simmer. Place two-thirds of the bittersweet chocolate in a heatproof bowl, place it over the simmering water, and stir until the chocolate has melted. Remove the pan from heat and let the chocolate cool.

2. In the work bowl of a stand mixer fitted with the paddle attachment, cream the butter, vanilla, and brown sugar on medium speed until the mixture is very light and fluffy, 2 to 3 minutes, scraping down the work bowl as necessary. Add the melted chocolate and beat to incorporate, again scraping down the work bowl as necessary.

3. Add the flour, cocoa powder, and salt and beat until the mixture comes together as a smooth dough. Add the milk chocolate and remaining bittersweet chocolate and beat until they are evenly distributed. Let the dough rest for 5 to 10 minutes.

4. Using a cookie scoop, drop 1 to 1½ oz. (30 to 45 g) portions of the dough on the pans, making sure to leave 2 inches between them. Place one pan of cookies in the oven at a time. Bake until their edges are set, 10 to 12 minutes, rotating the pans halfway through.

5. Remove the cookies from the oven and let them cool on the pans for a few minutes. Transfer the cookies to wire racks and let them cool completely before enjoying.

YIELD: 24 Cookies
ACTIVE TIME: 15 Minutes
TOTAL TIME: 3 Hours

WHITE CHOCOLATE & CRANBERRY COOKIES

An improbably good cookie, with the dried cranberries adding an extra bit of chewiness that pushes things into irresistible territory.

---

1. Preheat the oven to 350°F and line two sheet pans with parchment paper. In the work bowl of a stand mixer fitted with the paddle attachment, cream the butter, brown sugar, and sugar on medium speed until the mixture is very light and fluffy, 2 to 3 minutes, scraping down the work bowl as necessary.

2. Add the egg and beat until incorporated, again scraping the work bowl as necessary. When the egg has been incorporated, scrape down the work bowl, add the vanilla and beat to incorporate. Add the flour, baking soda, and salt and beat until the mixture comes together as a smooth dough. Add the white chocolate chips and cranberries and beat until they are evenly distributed. Let the dough rest for 5 to 10 minutes.

3. Using a cookie scoop, drop 1 to 1½ oz. (30 to 45 g) portions of the dough on the pans, making sure to leave 2 inches between them. Place one pan of cookies in the oven at a time. Bake until they are a light golden brown, 10 to 12 minutes, rotating the pans halfway through.

4. Remove the cookies from the oven and let them cool on the pans for a few minutes. Transfer the cookies to wire racks and let them cool completely before enjoying.

½ cup (113 g) unsalted butter, softened

1 cup (105 g) light brown sugar

½ cup (50 g) sugar

1 (50 g) egg

1 teaspoon (5 ml) pure vanilla extract

1½ cups (180 g) all-purpose flour

½ teaspoon (2 g) baking soda

½ teaspoon (3 g) table salt

¾ cup (155 g) white chocolate chips

½ cup (60 g) dried cranberries

YIELD: 36 Cookies

ACTIVE TIME: 20 Minutes

TOTAL TIME: 2 Hours

WHITE CHOCOLATE CHIP & MACADAMIA COOKIES

As far as nuts go, macadamias are the most buttery, making them an ideal pairing with creamy white chocolate.

1 cup (227 g) unsalted butter, softened

1 cup plus 2 tablespoons (225 g) sugar

1 cup plus 2 tablespoons (230 g) light brown sugar

2 (100 g) eggs

1½ teaspoons (7.5 ml) pure vanilla extract

3 (scant) cups (340 g) all-purpose flour

1½ teaspoons (9 g) table salt

1 teaspoon (4.5 g) baking soda

7 oz. (200 g) macadamia nuts, toasted

7 oz. (200 g) white chocolate chips

---

1. Preheat the oven to 350°F and line three sheet pans with parchment paper. In the work bowl of a stand mixer fitted with the paddle attachment, cream the butter, sugar, and brown sugar on medium speed until the mixture is very light and fluffy, 2 to 3 minutes, scraping down the work bowl as necessary.

2. Add the eggs one at a time and beat until incorporated, again scraping the work bowl as necessary. When the eggs have been incorporated, scrape down the work bowl, add the vanilla, and beat to incorporate. Add the flour, salt, and baking soda and beat until the mixture comes together as a smooth dough. Add the macadamia nuts and white chocolate chips and beat until they are evenly distributed. Let the dough rest for 5 to 10 minutes.

3. Using a cookie scoop, drop 1 to 1½ oz. (30 to 45 g) portions of the dough on the pans, making sure to leave 2 inches between them. Place one pan of cookies in the oven at a time. Bake until they are a light golden brown, 10 to 12 minutes, rotating the pans halfway through.

4. Remove the cookies from the oven and let them cool on the pans for a few minutes. Transfer the cookies to wire racks and let them cool completely before enjoying.

YIELD: 24 Cookies

ACTIVE TIME: 15 Minutes

TOTAL TIME: 1 Hour

ANISE & CHOCOLATE CHIP COOKIES

An anise-flavored liqueur can also be used in these cookies, if you prefer.

½ cup (113 g) unsalted butter, softened

½ cup (100 g) sugar

3 (150 g) eggs

¼ cup (57 g) whole milk

½ teaspoon (2.5 ml) pure vanilla extract

2 teaspoons (10 ml) anise extract

3 cups (360 g) all-purpose flour

½ teaspoon (3 g) table salt

2 teaspoons (9 g) baking powder

⅔ cup (115 g) semisweet chocolate chips

---

1. Preheat the oven to 350°F and line three sheet pans with parchment paper. In the work bowl of a stand mixer fitted with the paddle attachment, cream the butter and sugar on medium speed until the mixture is very light and fluffy, 2 to 3 minutes, scraping down the work bowl as necessary.
2. Add the eggs one at a time and beat until incorporated, again scraping the work bowl as necessary. When the eggs have been incorporated, scrape down the work bowl, add the milk, vanilla, and anise extract and beat to incorporate. Add the flour, salt, and baking powder and beat until the mixture comes together as a smooth dough. Add the chocolate chips and beat until they are evenly distributed. Let the dough rest for 5 to 10 minutes.
3. Using a cookie scoop, drop 2 oz. (60 g) portions of the dough on the pans, making sure to leave about 3 inches between each cookie. Place one pan of cookies in the oven at a time. Bake until they are golden brown, 12 to 14 minutes, rotating the pans halfway through.
4. Remove the cookies from the oven, transfer them to a wire rack, and let them cool completely before enjoying.

YIELD: 24 Cookies
ACTIVE TIME: 15 Minutes
TOTAL TIME: 1 Hour

CHOCOLATE, ORANGE & PECAN COOKIES

A cookie so good, it reminds us why the British flavor combination is beloved worldwide.

½ cup (113 g) unsalted butter, softened

½ cup (100 g) sugar

1 (50 g) egg

¼ cup (57 g) whole milk

Zest of 2 oranges

½ teaspoon (2.5 ml) pure vanilla extract

1½ cups (180 g) all-purpose flour

½ teaspoon (3 g) table salt

2 teaspoons (9 g) baking powder

⅔ cup (115 g) semisweet chocolate chips

½ cup (50 g) pecans, chopped

---

1. In the work bowl of a stand mixer fitted with the paddle attachment, cream the butter and sugar on medium speed until the mixture is very light and fluffy, 2 to 3 minutes, scraping down the work bowl as necessary.
2. Add the egg and beat until it is incorporated, again scraping the work bowl as necessary. When the egg has been incorporated, scrape down the work bowl, add the orange zest and vanilla and beat to incorporate. Add the flour, salt, and baking powder and beat until the mixture comes together as a smooth dough. Add the chocolate chips and pecans and beat until they are evenly distributed. Let the dough rest for 5 to 10 minutes.
3. Using a cookie scoop, drop 1 to 1½ oz. (30 to 45 g) portions of the dough on the pans, making sure to leave about 2 inches between each cookie. Place one pan of cookies in the oven at a time. Bake until they are golden brown, 12 to 14 minutes, rotating the pans halfway through.
4. Remove the cookies from the oven, transfer them to a wire rack, and let them cool completely before enjoying.

YIELD: 20 Cookies

ACTIVE TIME: 30 Minutes

TOTAL TIME: 2 Hours and 15 Minutes

CHOCOLATE SANDWICH COOKIES

Inspired by the Oreo, this version proves once and for all that homemade is superior to store-bought.

1 cup (227 g) unsalted butter, softened

2¼ cups (450 g) sugar

2 (100 g) eggs

¾ teaspoon (3.5 ml) pure vanilla extract

2¼ cups (270 g) all-purpose flour

1½ cups (125 g) cocoa powder

2 teaspoons (8 g) baking powder

¾ teaspoon (4 g) kosher salt

1 cup (225 g) Butterfluff Filling (see page 354)

---

1. Preheat the oven to 350°F and line two sheet pans with parchment paper. In the work bowl of a stand mixer fitted with the paddle attachment, cream the butter and sugar on medium speed until the mixture is very light and fluffy, 2 to 3 minutes, scraping down the work bowl as necessary.

2. Reduce the speed to low, add the eggs one at a time, and beat until incorporated, again scraping the work bowl as needed. When both eggs have been incorporated, scrape down the work bowl, add the vanilla, and beat for another minute. Add the flour, cocoa powder, baking powder, and salt and beat on low until the mixture comes together as a dough. Let the dough rest for 5 to 10 minutes.

3. Using a cookie scoop, drop 1 to 1½ oz. (30 to 45 g) portions of the dough on the pans, making sure to leave about 2 inches between each cookie. Coat the bottom of a measuring cup with nonstick cooking spray and use it to gently press down on each cookie, flattening them.

4. Place one pan of cookies in the oven at a time. Bake until they are dry to the touch, 12 to 14 minutes, rotating the pans halfway through. Remove the cookies from the oven, transfer them to a wire rack, and let them cool completely.

5. Place the filling in a piping bag and cut a ½-inch hole in the bag. Pipe about 1 tablespoon of filling on half of the cookies. Use the other half to assemble the sandwich cookies and enjoy.

CUT IT OUT

When the time comes to supply a loved one with quick comfort or articulate the glory of a specific season or holiday, the recipes in this chapter are where you'll turn. Defined by crisp edges, eye-catching shapes, and indelible memories, making cut-out cookies is perhaps the most rewarding time one can spend in the kitchen, redolent with the warmth of home.

YIELD: 16 Cookies
ACTIVE TIME: 15 Minutes
TOTAL TIME: 2 Hours

HAZELNUT & MOCHA TOWERS

A fun, eye-catching cookie that looks far more impressive than the efforts that are actually required to produce it.

---

1 cup (227 g) unsalted butter, softened

1¼ cups (250 g) sugar

1 (50 g) egg

1 (15 g) egg yolk

2 teaspoons (10 ml) pure vanilla extract

4 teaspoons (8 g) instant espresso powder

2½ cups (300 g) all-purpose flour, plus more as needed

½ teaspoon (2 g) table salt

½ teaspoon (2 g) baking powder

1 cup (135 g) finely ground hazelnuts

Chocolate Ganache (see page 351), warm

1. In the work bowl of a stand mixer fitted with the paddle attachment, cream the butter and sugar on medium speed until the mixture is very light and fluffy, 2 to 3 minutes, scraping down the work bowl as necessary.

2. Add the egg, egg yolk, and vanilla and beat to incorporate, again scraping the work bowl as necessary. Add the espresso powder, flour, salt, and baking powder and beat until the mixture comes together as a shaggy dough. Add the ground hazelnuts and beat until the mixture comes together as a smooth dough. Divide the dough into three pieces, cover the dough with plastic wrap, and chill it in the refrigerator for 1 hour.

3. Preheat the oven to 375°F and line three sheet pans with parchment paper. Place the dough on a flour-dusted work surface and roll out each piece to about ¼ inch thick. Cut each piece of dough into 1 x 3–inch rectangles and arrange them on sheet pans, making sure to leave 1 inch between them.

4. Place one pan of cookies in the oven at a time. Bake until they are crispy and dry to the touch, 10 to 12 minutes, rotating the pans halfway through. Remove the cookies from the oven and let them cool on the pans for a few minutes before transferring them to wire racks to cool completely.

5. Spread the ganache over two-thirds of the cookies. Stack them in towers of three cookies, with the ganache-less cookies sitting on top, and enjoy.

YIELD: 48 Cookies
ACTIVE TIME: 40 Minutes
TOTAL TIME: 3 Hours

CLASSIC SUGAR COOKIES

Of course, sugar cookies are always abundant around the holidays. But in truth they're wonderful any time of year—particularly when made with a loved one.

1 cup (227 g) unsalted butter, softened

1 cup (210 g) light brown sugar

1 (50 g) egg

2⅘ cups (340 g) all-purpose flour, plus more as needed

1 teaspoon (4 g) baking powder

½ teaspoon (2.5 g) table salt

Royal Icing (see page 353), to decorate

---

1. In the work bowl of a stand mixer fitted with the paddle attachment, cream the butter and brown sugar on medium speed until the mixture is very light and fluffy, 2 to 3 minutes, scraping down the work bowl as necessary.
2. Add the egg and beat until incorporated, again scraping the work bowl as necessary. When the egg has been incorporated, scrape down the work bowl, add the flour, baking powder, and salt, and beat until the mixture comes together as a smooth dough. Cover the dough with plastic wrap and chill it in the refrigerator for 2 hours.
3. Preheat the oven to 350°F and line three sheet pans with parchment paper. Place the dough on a flour-dusted work surface and roll it out until it is approximately ¼ inch thick. Use cookie cutters to cut the dough into the desired shapes and place them on the pans, making sure to leave 1 inch between them.
4. Place one pan of cookies in the oven at a time and chill the other cookies in the refrigerator. Bake until their edges are lightly golden brown, 8 to 10 minutes, rotating the pans halfway through. Remove the cookies from the oven, transfer them to a wire rack, and let them cool completely.
5. Decorate the cookies with the icing and let it set before enjoying.

CLASSIC SUGAR COOKIES

page 127

YIELD: 50 Tozzetti

ACTIVE TIME: 30 Minutes

TOTAL TIME: 1 Hour

TOZZETTI

Tozzetti are the Umbrian version of Tuscany's famed cantucci. Truth is, this type of cookie is very common in several regions of Italy, including Sicily, where they are called pepatelli.

3⅓ cups (400 g) all-purpose flour

1½ teaspoons (6 g) baker's ammonia (ammonium carbonate)

Pinch of table salt

3 (150 g) eggs

1 cup (200 g) sugar

Zest of 1½ oranges

Zest of 1½ lemons

½ teaspoon (1 g) anise seeds

½ cup (60 g) hazelnuts, chopped

¼ cup (40 g) raisins

2½ tablespoons (20 g) pine nuts

¼ cup (45 g) candied fruit, diced

---

1. Preheat the oven to 350°F and line a sheet pan with parchment paper. In a large bowl, combine the flour, baker's ammonia, and salt. In the work bowl of a stand mixer fitted with the paddle attachment, beat the eggs and sugar on medium speed until well combined. Add the citrus zests and anise seeds and beat to incorporate.
2. With the mixer running, gradually add the flour mixture until the mixture just comes together as a smooth dough. Add the hazelnuts, raisins, pine nuts, and candied fruit and beat until they are evenly distributed. Divide the dough into three pieces and shape each one into a 1½-inch-wide log.
3. Place the logs on the pan and place them in the oven. Bake for about 20 minutes, remove the tozzetti from the oven, and cut each log into ⅔-inch-thick slices. Place the tozzetti back on the pan, cut side up, and return them to the oven. Bake for 10 minutes, turning the tozzetti over halfway through.
4. Remove them from the oven, transfer them to a wire rack, and let them cool completely before serving.

YIELD: 36 Cookies

ACTIVE TIME: 15 Minutes

TOTAL TIME: 3 Hours

SMASHED PUMPKIN COOKIE

Despite what the cheeky name implies, you don't worry have to worry about being overserved here—the alcohol in the Cognac will cook off in the oven.

¾ cup (170 g) unsalted butter, softened

½ cup (100 g) sugar

1 teaspoon (5 ml) pure vanilla extract

1 (15 g) egg yolk

2 tablespoons (30 ml) Cognac

Pinch of freshly grated nutmeg

3 cups (360 g) all-purpose flour

Royal Icing (see page 353)

1 drop of orange gel food coloring

1 drop of black gel food coloring

---

1. In the work bowl of a stand mixer fitted with the paddle attachment, cream the butter and sugar on medium speed until the mixture is very light and fluffy, 2 to 3 minutes, scraping down the work bowl as necessary.
2. Add the vanilla, egg yolk, Cognac, and nutmeg and beat until incorporated, again scraping down the work bowl as necessary. Add the flour and beat the mixture until it comes together as a smooth dough. Divide the dough in half, place each piece between two sheets of parchment paper, and roll out to ¼ inch thick. Chill the dough in the refrigerator for 2 hours.
3. Preheat the oven to 350°F and line three sheet pans with parchment paper. Using pumpkin-shaped cookie cutters, cut cookies out of the dough and arrange them on the pans, making sure to leave 1 inch between them. Place one pan of cookies in the oven at a time. Bake until their edges start to brown, 10 to 12 minutes, rotating the pans halfway through.
4. Remove the cookies from the oven and let them cool on the pans for a few minutes before transferring them to wire racks to cool completely.
5. Divide the icing in half and place each portion in its own bowl. Stir the orange food coloring into one portion and the black food coloring into the other. Decorate the cookies with the icing as desired and let it set before enjoying.

YIELD: 50 Cantucci
ACTIVE TIME: 30 Minutes
TOTAL TIME: 1 Hour

CANTUCCI

Cantucci are probably the most internationally renowned Italian cookies. Originally made in Tuscany, they became famous in the nineteenth century, when a pastry chef from Prato refined the recipe and presented them at 1867 World's Fair in Paris.

- 3⅓ cups (400 g) all-purpose flour
- 1½ teaspoons (6 g) baker's ammonia (ammonium carbonate)
- Pinch of table salt
- 3 (150 g) eggs
- 1 cup (200 g) sugar
- Zest of 1½ oranges
- Zest of 1½ lemons
- 1 teaspoon (5 ml) pure vanilla extract
- 1¼ cups (145 g) silvered almonds

---

1. Preheat the oven to 350°F and line a sheet pan with parchment paper. In a large bowl, combine the flour, baker's ammonia, and salt. In the work bowl of a stand mixer fitted with the paddle attachment, beat the eggs and sugar on medium speed until well combined. Add the citrus zests and vanilla and beat to incorporate.
2. With the mixer running, gradually add the flour mixture until the mixture just comes together as a smooth dough. Add the almonds and beat until they are evenly distributed. Divide the dough into three pieces and shape each one into a 1½-inch-wide log.
3. Place the logs on the pan and place them in the oven. Bake for about 20 minutes, remove the cantucci from the oven, and cut each log into ⅔-inch-thick slices. Place the cantucci back on the pan, cut side up, and return them to the oven. Bake for 10 minutes, turning the cantucci over halfway through.
4. Remove them from the oven, transfer them to a wire rack, and let them cool completely before serving.

YIELD: 60 Cookies
ACTIVE TIME: 15 Minutes
TOTAL TIME: 1 Hour and 45 Minutes

A STAR IS BORN

The almond meal adds richness and texture to these biscuity cookies.

1 cup (227 g) unsalted butter, softened

1⅓ cups (265 g) sugar

1 teaspoon (5 ml) pure vanilla extract

2 (100 g) eggs

2 (30 g) egg yolks

½ teaspoon (1 g) cinnamon

Pinch of ground nutmeg

1 cup (84 g) almond meal

3½ cups (420 g) all-purpose flour, plus more for dusting

Vanilla Glaze (see page 351), to top

---

1. In the work bowl of a stand mixer fitted with the paddle attachment, cream the butter, sugar, vanilla, eggs, and egg yolks on medium speed until the mixture is very light and fluffy, 2 to 3 minutes, scraping down the work bowl as necessary.

2. Add the cinnamon and nutmeg, beat to incorporate, and then add the almond meal and flour. Beat until the mixture comes together as a smooth dough. Cover the dough in plastic wrap and chill it in the refrigerator for 1 hour.

3. Preheat the oven to 350°F and line three sheet pans with parchment paper. Place the dough on a flour-dusted work surface and roll it out to ⅛ inch thick. Use cookie cutters to cut the dough into star shapes and place them on the pans, making sure to leave 1 inch between them. Place one pan of cookies in the oven at a time. Bake until they are a light golden brown, 8 to 10 minutes, rotating the pans halfway through.

4. Remove the cookies from the oven, transfer them to wire racks, and let them cool completely. When the cookies have cooled, top them with Vanilla Glaze and let it set before enjoying.

YIELD: 36 Cookies
ACTIVE TIME: 15 Minutes
TOTAL TIME: 2 Hours

PEANUT & POPPY SEED COOKIES

If you want a bit more sweetness here, add a ½ cup of white chocolate chips.

- ½ cup (113 g) unsalted butter, softened
- ½ cup (105 g) light brown sugar
- ½ cup (100 g) sugar
- 1 (50 g) egg
- 1 teaspoon (5 ml) pure vanilla extract
- ⅔ cup (80 g) all-purpose flour, plus more as needed
- ½ cup (50 g) almond flour
- ¼ teaspoon (1 g) table salt
- ½ teaspoon (2 g) baking soda
- 1 cup (140 g) peanuts, chopped
- 1 cup (130 g) poppy seeds

---

1. In the work bowl of a stand mixer fitted with the paddle attachment, cream the butter, brown sugar, and sugar on medium speed until the mixture is very light and fluffy, 2 to 3 minutes, scraping down the work bowl as necessary.
2. Add the egg and beat until incorporated, again scraping the work bowl as necessary. When the egg has been incorporated, scrape down the work bowl, add the vanilla, and beat to incorporate. Add the flours, salt, and baking soda, and beat until the mixture comes together as a smooth dough. Add the peanuts and poppy seeds and beat until they are evenly distributed. Divide the dough in half, form each piece of dough into a log, and cover them with plastic wrap. Let the dough chill in the refrigerator for 1 hour.
3. Preheat the oven to 350°F and line three sheet pans with parchment paper. Cut the logs into ½-inch-thick slices and place them on the pans, making sure to leave 1 inch between them. Place one pan of cookies in the oven at a time. Bake until they are a light golden brown, 8 to 10 minutes, rotating the pans halfway through.
4. Remove the cookies from the oven, transfer them to wire racks, and let them cool completely before enjoying.

¾ cup plus 1 tablespoon (185 g) unsalted butter, softened

¾ cup plus ¼ cup (150 g) sugar

2 tablespoons (30 ml) unsweetened almond milk

1 tablespoon (7 g) cornstarch

1 teaspoon (5 ml) pure vanilla extract

2¼ cups (270 g) all-purpose flour, plus more as needed

½ teaspoon (2 g) baking powder

½ teaspoon (3 g) table salt

2 small Braeburn apples, peeled, cored, and diced

1 teaspoon (3 g) cinnamon

Caramel Sauce (see page 354)

YIELD: 36 Cookies
ACTIVE TIME: 15 Minutes
TOTAL TIME: 2 Hours

CARAMEL APPLE COOKIES

All of the flavors and fun available at the state fair, without having to battle the crowds.

---

1. In the work bowl of a stand mixer fitted with the paddle attachment, cream ¾ cup of butter and ¾ cup of sugar on medium speed until the mixture is very light and fluffy, 2 to 3 minutes, scraping down the work bowl as necessary.
2. Add the almond milk, cornstarch, and vanilla and beat until incorporated, again scraping down the work bowl as necessary. Add the flour, baking powder, and salt and beat until the mixture comes together as a firm dough. Form the dough into a disk, cover it with plastic wrap, and chill it in the refrigerator for 1 hour.
3. Preheat the oven to 350°F and line two sheet pans with parchment paper. Place the dough on a flour-dusted work surface and roll it out to about ¼ inch thick. Using cookie cutters, cut the dough into the desired shapes and arrange them on the pans, making sure to leave 1 inch between them. Make a slight indentation in the center of each cookie. Place one pan of cookies in the oven at a time. Bake until they are a light golden brown at the edges, 10 to 12 minutes, rotating the pans halfway through.
4. Remove the cookies from the oven and let them cool on the pans for a few minutes before transferring to wire racks to cool completely.
5. Place the remaining butter in a large skillet and melt it over medium heat. Add the apples, sprinkle the cinnamon and remaining sugar over them, and cook, stirring, until the apples are tender and the mixture has thickened. Remove the pan from heat and let the mixture cool.
6. Spoon about 1 teaspoon of the apple mixture into the indentations in the cookies. Drizzle the caramel over the cookies and let it set before enjoying.

YIELD: 24 Cookies
ACTIVE TIME: 20 Minutes
TOTAL TIME: 1 Hour

CHAI COOKIES

Tea time just became a little bit more intriguing.

2 bags of chai tea

1 cup (227 g) unsalted butter, softened

½ cup (60 g) confectioners' sugar

1 teaspoon (5 ml) pure vanilla extract

2 cups (240 g) all-purpose flour, plus more as needed

2 tablespoons (15 g) cornstarch

½ teaspoon (3 g) table salt

---

1. Preheat the oven to 350°F and line two sheet pans with parchment paper. Carefully cut the tops of the tea bags off. Pour the tea into a small bowl and set it aside.
2. In the work bowl of a stand mixer fitted with the paddle attachment, cream the butter and confectioners' sugar on medium speed until the mixture is very light and fluffy, 2 to 3 minutes, scraping down the work bowl as necessary. Add the vanilla and beat to incorporate. Add the flour, cornstarch, and salt and beat until the mixture comes together as a smooth dough. Add the tea and beat until it is evenly distributed.
3. Place the dough on a flour-dusted work surface and roll it out to about ¼ inch thick. Cut the dough into rounds, arrange them on the pans, making sure to leave 1 inch between them, and prick the cookies with a fork. Place one pan of cookies in the oven at a time. Bake until they are golden brown and their edges are set, 12 to 14 minutes, rotating the pans halfway through.
4. Remove the cookies from the oven and let them cool on the pans for a few minutes. Transfer the cookies to wire racks and let them cool completely before enjoying.

YIELD: 36 Cookies

ACTIVE TIME: 30 Minutes

TOTAL TIME: 3 Hours and 30 Minutes

CHOCOLATE-COVERED MARSHMALLOW COOKIES

Marshmallows add their famed lusciousness to these indulgent treats.

2¾ cups (330 g) all-purpose flour, plus more as needed

⅔ cup (135 g) sugar

½ teaspoon (2 g) table salt

1 teaspoon (4 g) baking powder

1 teaspoon (2 g) cinnamon

¾ cup (170 g) unsalted butter, divided into tablespoons

3 (150 g) eggs, lightly beaten

12 large marshmallows, cut into thirds

Coating Chocolate (see page 352), to top

1. Place the flour, sugar, salt, baking powder, and cinnamon in a mixing bowl and whisk to combine. Add the butter and work the mixture with a pastry cutter until it resembles coarse bread crumbs. Add the eggs and stir until the mixture comes together as a smooth dough. Shape the dough into a ball, cover it with plastic wrap, and chill it in the refrigerator for 1 hour.

2. Preheat the oven to 375°F and line two sheet pans with parchment paper. Place the dough on a flour-dusted work surface and roll it out to about ¼ inch thick. Cut the dough into rounds and arrange them on the pans, making sure to leave 1 inch between them. Place one pan of cookies in the oven at a time. Bake until their edges are a light golden brown, 10 to 12 minutes, rotating the pans halfway through.

3. Remove the cookies from the oven and let them cool on the pans for a few minutes. Place a piece of marshmallow on each cookie. Place them back in the oven and, while keeping a close eye on the cookies, bake until marshmallows start to collapse. Remove the cookies from the oven and let them cool completely on the pans.

4. Drizzle the Coating Chocolate over the cookies until they are completely covered and let it set before enjoying.

YIELD: 24 Cookies

ACTIVE TIME: 15 Minutes

TOTAL TIME: 1 Hour and 30 Minutes

LINZER COOKIES

The flavors in Austria's famed pastry work just as well in cookie form.

1 cup (227 g) unsalted butter, softened

1 cup (113 g) confectioners' sugar, plus more to top

3 (45 g) egg yolks

1 teaspoon (5 ml) almond extract

3½ cups (420 g) all-purpose flour, plus more as needed

1 tablespoon (15 ml) whole milk

½ cup (170 g) raspberry jam

---

1. In the work bowl of a stand mixer fitted with the paddle attachment, cream the butter and confectioners' sugar on medium speed until the mixture is very light and fluffy, 2 to 3 minutes, scraping down the work bowl as necessary.
2. Add the egg yolks and almond extract and beat to incorporate, again scraping the work bowl as necessary. Add the flour and beat until the mixture comes together as a shaggy dough. Gradually add the milk and beat until the dough is smooth. Form the dough into a disk, cover it with plastic wrap, and chill the dough in the refrigerator for 30 minutes.
3. Preheat the oven to 350°F and line three sheet pans with parchment paper. Roll the dough out on a flour-dusted work surface until it is about ⅛ inch thick. Cut the dough into 1½-inch rounds, use smaller cookie cutters to cut designs in the centers of half of the cookies, and then arrange all of the cookies on the pans, making sure to leave 1 inch between them.
4. Place one pan of cookies in the oven at a time. Bake until their edges are a light golden brown, 10 to 12 minutes, rotating the pans halfway through. Remove the cookies from the oven and let them cool on the pans for a few minutes. Transfer the cookies to wire racks and let them cool completely.
5. Spread some of the raspberry jam on the cookies without any designs cut into them. Assemble the sandwiches with the other cookies and enjoy.

YIELD: 24 Cookies

ACTIVE TIME: 15 Minutes

TOTAL TIME: 2 Hours

¾ cup (170 g) unsalted butter, softened

⅓ cup (65 g) sugar, plus more to top

1⅓ cups (160 g) all-purpose flour

Pinch of table salt

3 tablespoons (15 g) cocoa powder

CHOCOLATE TEA COOKIES

Earl Grey and Lapsang souchong are great tea pairings for this cookie.

---

1. In the work bowl of a stand mixer fitted with the paddle attachment, cream the butter and sugar on medium speed until the mixture is very light and fluffy, 2 to 3 minutes, scraping down the work bowl as necessary. Add the flour, salt, and cocoa powder and beat until the mixture comes together as a smooth dough. Divide the dough in half and roll each piece into a 2-inch-thick log. Cover the dough in plastic wrap and chill it in the refrigerator for 1 hour.
2. Preheat the oven to 350°F and line two sheet pans with parchment paper. Cut the logs into ¼-inch-thick slices and arrange them on the pans, making sure to leave 1 inch between them. Sprinkle additional sugar over the top.
3. Place one pan of cookies in the oven at a time. Bake until they are golden brown and dry to the touch, 10 to 12 minutes, rotating the pans halfway through.
4. Remove the cookies from the oven and let them cool on the pans before enjoying.

YIELD: 24 Cookies
ACTIVE TIME: 15 Minutes
TOTAL TIME: 3 Hours

CINNAMON SWIRL COOKIES

The key here is rolling up the dough as tight as you can to produce cookies featuring a mesmerizing swirl.

2 cups (240 g) all-purpose flour, plus more as needed

⅓ cup plus ¼ cup (115 g) sugar

Pinch of table salt

⅔ cup (150 g) unsalted butter, softened and cubed; plus 2 tablespoons (25 g), melted

¼ cup (55 g) cream cheese, softened

1 (15 g) egg yolk

1 teaspoon (5 ml) pure vanilla extract

1 tablespoon (9 g) cinnamon

---

1. Sift the flour, ⅓ cup of sugar, and salt into a mixing bowl. Add the softened butter and work the mixture with a pastry cutter until it resembles coarse bread crumbs. Add the cream cheese, egg yolk, and vanilla and knead the mixture until it comes together as a smooth dough. Form the dough into a disk, cover it with plastic wrap, and chill it in the refrigerator for 1 hour.

2. Place the dough on a flour-dusted work surface and roll it out until it is an approximately 8 x 10–inch rectangle. Brush it with the melted butter. Combine the cinnamon and the remaining sugar and sprinkle the mixture over the dough. Roll the dough into a tight cylinder, cover it with plastic wrap, and chill it in the refrigerator for another hour.

3. Preheat the oven to 350°F and line two sheet pans with parchment paper. Cut the dough into ¼-inch-thick slices and arrange them on the pans, making sure to leave 1 inch between them.

4. Place one pan of cookies in the oven at a time. Bake until they are golden brown and their edges are set, 10 to 12 minutes, rotating the pans halfway through.

5. Remove the cookies from the oven and let them cool on the pans for a few minutes. Transfer the cookies to wire racks and let them cool completely before enjoying.

YIELD: 24 Cookies
ACTIVE TIME: 25 Minutes
TOTAL TIME: 2 Hours

¾ cup (170 g) unsalted butter, melted

⅓ cup (65 g) sugar

2½ cups (300 g) all-purpose flour, plus more as needed

Pinch of table salt

½ teaspoon (2 g) baking powder

EASY LATTICE COOKIES

These cookies come with a flavor that matches their distinguished look.

---

1. Place all of the ingredients in the work bowl of a stand mixer fitted with the paddle attachment and beat until the mixture comes together as a smooth dough. Shape the dough into a disk, cover it with plastic wrap, and chill it in the refrigerator for 1 hour.

2. Preheat the oven to 350°F and line two sheet pans with parchment paper. Place the dough on a flour-dusted work surface and roll it out to about ¼ inch thick. Cut the dough into rounds and arrange them on the pans, making sure to leave 1 inch between them. Working with a sharp paring knife, cut out lattice patterns from each piece of dough; if necessary, use a cardboard stencil pattern on top of the dough to help cut out the patterns, or a lace pattern cookie cutter.

3. Place one pan of cookies in the oven at a time. Bake until they are starting to firm up, 12 to 14 minutes, rotating the pans halfway through.

4. Remove the cookies from the oven and let them cool on the pans for a few minutes. Transfer the cookies to wire racks and let them cool completely before enjoying.

YIELD: 15 Cookies

ACTIVE TIME: 15 Minutes

TOTAL TIME: 2 Hours

PISTACHIO & FENNEL BISCUITS

Fennel's flavor develops considerably in the oven, a quality that enhances these warming, comforting cookies.

½ cup (113 g) unsalted butter, softened

¼ cup (50 g) sugar

¾ cup (90 g) all-purpose flour, plus more as needed

⅓ cup (30 g) almond flour

2 teaspoons (2 g) fennel seeds, finely ground

¼ cup (30 g) chopped shelled pistachios

---

1. In the work bowl of a stand mixer fitted with the paddle attachment, cream the butter and sugar on medium speed until the mixture is very light and fluffy, 2 to 3 minutes, scraping down the work bowl as necessary.
2. Add the flours and fennel seeds and beat until the mixture comes together as a smooth dough. Form the dough into a disk, cover it with plastic wrap, and chill it in the refrigerator for 1 hour.
3. Preheat the oven to 350°F and line two sheet pans with parchment paper. Place the dough on a flour-dusted work surface and roll out to ⅓ inch thick. Cut the cookies into rounds, arrange them on the pans, making sure to leave 1 inch between them, and sprinkle some pistachios on top of each cookie.
4. Place one pan of cookies in the oven at a time. Bake until they are just golden brown, 10 to 12 minutes, rotating the pans halfway through.
5. Remove the cookies from the oven and let them cool on the pans for a few minutes. Transfer the cookies to a wire rack and let them cool completely before enjoying.

YIELD: 18 Cookies

ACTIVE TIME: 15 Minutes

TOTAL TIME: 1 Hour and 30 Minutes

LEMON & RICE FLOUR SHORTBREAD

A gluten-free shortbread so good that no one will take note of gluten's absence.

1 cup (227 g) unsalted butter, softened

¾ cup (150 g) sugar

1 tablespoon (6 g) lemon zest

2 cups (310 g) gluten-free all-purpose flour, plus more as needed

1 cup (140 g) rice flour

---

1. In the work bowl of a stand mixer fitted with the paddle attachment, cream the butter, sugar, and lemon zest on medium speed until the mixture is very light and fluffy, 2 to 3 minutes, scraping down the work bowl as necessary.
2. Gradually add the flours and beat until the mixture comes together as a smooth dough. Form the dough into a disk, cover it with parchment paper, and chill it in the refrigerator for 30 minutes.
3. Preheat the oven to 350°F and line two sheet pans with parchment paper. Place the dough on a flour-dusted work surface and roll it out to ⅛ inch thick. Cut the dough into 1½-inch rounds and place them on the pans, making sure to leave 1 inch between them.
4. Place one pan of cookies in the oven at a time. Bake until they are a light golden brown, 10 to 12 minutes, rotating the pans halfway through.
5. Remove the cookies from the oven and let them cool on the pans for a few minutes. Transfer the cookies to a wire rack and let them cool completely before enjoying.

YIELD: 24 Cookies
ACTIVE TIME: 30 Minutes
TOTAL TIME: 1 Hour and 45 Minutes

GLUTEN-FREE SUGAR COOKIES

Nutty and slightly earthy, amaranth flour has the power to make even the most traditional bakers rethink the possibilities of gluten-free options.

1½ cups (150 g) amaranth flour

1 cup (113 g) confectioners' sugar

½ cup (55 g) cornstarch

1 teaspoon (2 g) xanthan gum

1 teaspoon (3 g) cream of tartar

Pinch of table salt

1 cup (227 g) unsalted butter, cut into thin slices

1 (50 g) egg

1 tablespoon (15 ml) whole milk

1 teaspoon (5 ml) pure vanilla extract

Glutinous rice flour, as needed

Vanilla Glaze (see page 351), to top

Colored sugars, to decorate (optional)

---

1. Place the amaranth flour, confectioners' sugar, cornstarch, xanthan gum, cream of tartar, and salt in a food processor and blitz until combined. Add the butter and pulse until the mixture resembles coarse bread crumbs.

2. Place the egg, milk, and vanilla in a small cup and whisk to combine. Drizzle the mixture into the food processor and pulse until the resulting mixture comes together as a stiff dough. Divide the dough in half, cover it with parchment paper, and flatten it into disks. Chill the dough in the refrigerator for 1 hour.

3. Preheat the oven to 350°F and line two sheet pans with parchment paper. Dust a sheet of parchment paper and a rolling pin with sweet rice flour. Place the dough on the parchment paper and roll it out to a ¼ inch thick. Repeat the process with the other disk. Use cookie cutters to cut the dough into the desired shapes and place them on the pans, making sure to leave 1 inch between them.

4. Place one pan of cookies in the oven at a time. Bake until their edges start to brown, 10 to 12 minutes, rotating the pans halfway through. Remove the cookies from the oven and let them cool on the pans for a few minutes before transferring them a wire rack to cool completely.

5. Spread the glaze over the cookies and decorate them with colored sugars (if desired). Let the glaze set before enjoying.

GLUTEN-FREE SUGAR COOKIES

page 157

YIELD: 24 Cookies
ACTIVE TIME: 1 Hour and 30 Minutes
TOTAL TIME: 4 Hours

GRASSHOPPER COOKIES

Mint's famed friendship with chocolate is never on stronger footing than it is in these cookies.

1 cup (227 g) unsalted butter

¼ cup (60 g) sugar

1 (15 g) egg yolk, at room temperature

½ teaspoon (2.5 ml) pure vanilla extract

½ teaspoon (2.5 ml) peppermint extract

½ teaspoon (2 g) baking powder

½ teaspoon (2 g) table salt

½ cup (40 g) cocoa powder

2 cups (240 g) all-purpose flour

Chocolate Ganache (see page 351), warm

---

1. In the work bowl of a stand mixer fitted with the paddle attachment, cream the butter and sugar on medium speed until the mixture is very light and fluffy, 2 to 3 minutes, scraping down the work bowl as necessary.
2. Add the egg yolk, vanilla, and peppermint extract and beat until incorporated, again scraping down the work bowl as necessary. Add the baking powder, salt, cocoa powder, and flour and beat the mixture until it comes together as a stiff dough. Place the dough on a sheet of parchment paper and roll it into a 2½-inch-thick log. Chill the dough in the refrigerator for 2 hours.
3. Preheat the oven to 350°F and line two sheet pans with parchment paper. Cut the chilled dough into ½-inch-thick slices and place them on the pans, making sure to leave 1 inch between them. Place one pan of cookies in the oven at a time. Bake until the edges start to firm up, 8 to 10 minutes.
4. Remove the cookies from the oven and let them cool on the pans for a few minutes before transferring them to wire racks to cool completely.
5. Dip the cookies in the ganache until they are completely coated and place them back on the pans. Chill the cookies in the refrigerator until the chocolate has hardened before enjoying.

1¼ cups (285 g) unsalted butter, softened

1 cup plus 2 tablespoons (240 g) light brown sugar

¼ cup (85 ml) honey

Zest of 1 orange

6 (85 g) egg yolks

2 tablespoons (30 ml) orange juice

4¼ cups (510 g) all-purpose flour, plus more as needed

1¼ teaspoons (6 g) baking soda

½ teaspoon (1 g) cinnamon

½ teaspoon (2 g) table salt

6 cups (2040 g) fig preserves or jam

YIELD: 60 Cookies
ACTIVE TIME: 1 Hour
TOTAL TIME: 2 Hours and 30 Minutes

FIG CAKE COOKIES

When a Fig Newton gets the homemade treatment, it becomes even more delicious.

---

1. In the work bowl of a stand mixer fitted with the paddle attachment, cream the butter, brown sugar, honey, and orange zest on medium speed until the mixture is very light and fluffy, 2 to 3 minutes, scraping down the work bowl as necessary.

2. Add the egg yolks and orange juice, and beat to incorporate, again scraping down the work bowl as necessary. Add the flour, baking soda, cinnamon, and salt and beat until the mixture comes together as a smooth dough. Place the dough on a flour-dusted work surface and divide it into two 6-inch squares. Cover each piece with plastic wrap and chill the dough in the refrigerator for 1 hour.

3. Preheat the oven to 350°F and line three sheet pans with parchment paper. Place one piece of dough on a flour-dusted work surface and roll out until it is a 15-inch square. Cut the dough into 3-inch-wide strips. Place the preserves in a piping bag and cut a 1-inch hole in it. Pipe a strip of filling down the center of each strip of dough, leaving 1 inch on either side. Gently fold the dough over the filling so that it is sealed. Flip the strips over so that the seams are facing down. Transfer the cookies to the pans, place them back in the refrigerator, and let them chill for 10 minutes. Repeat with the remaining piece of dough and fig preserves.

4. Cut the strips into 2-inch squares and place them back on the pans, making sure to leave 1 inch between them. Place one pan of cookies in the oven at a time. Bake until they are golden brown, 10 to 12 minutes, rotating the pans halfway through.

5. Remove the cookies from the oven and let them cool on the pans for a few minutes. Transfer the cookies to wire racks and let them cool completely before enjoying.

YIELD: 12 Cookies

ACTIVE TIME: 15 Minutes

TOTAL TIME: 1 Hour

2½ tablespoons (30 g) unsalted butter

5 (250 g) eggs, whites and yolks separated

¼ teaspoon (1 ml) fresh lemon juice

Pinch of table salt

½ cup (100 g) sugar

1 teaspoon (5 ml) pure vanilla extract

Zest of ½ lemon

¾ cup (90 g) all-purpose flour

¼ cup (28 g) cornstarch

½ teaspoon (2 g) baking powder

⅔ cup (225 g) raspberry jam

LEMON & RASPBERRY HEARTS

Whipping the egg whites before adding them to the dough results in an improbably light and airy cookie.

---

1. Preheat the oven to 425°F and line a sheet pan with parchment paper, making sure it hangs over the short ends of the pan. Place the butter in a small saucepan and melt it over low heat. Remove the pan from heat and set it aside.
2. In a mixing bowl, whip the egg whites, lemon juice, and salt until the mixture holds stiff peaks. Cover the bowl with plastic wrap and chill it in the refrigerator.
3. In the work bowl of a stand mixer fitted with the paddle attachment, beat the egg yolks, sugar, and vanilla until the mixture is thick and pale. Add the lemon zest, beat to incorporate, and add the egg whites in three increments, folding to incorporate. Sift the flour, cornstarch, and baking powder into the bowl, add the melted butter, and beat until the mixture comes together as a smooth batter.
4. Spread the mixture evenly in the pan, place it in the oven, and bake until it is golden brown and set, 10 to 12 minutes, rotating the pan halfway through. Remove the cookie from the oven and remove it from the pan by lifting it out by the parchment paper. Transfer the cookie to a wire rack and let it cool completely.
5. Using a small heart-shaped cookie cutter, cut 24 smaller cookies out of the cookie. Warm the jam in a small saucepan, spread it over half of the cookies, assemble the sandwiches with the remaining cookies, and enjoy.

YIELD: 40 Cookies
ACTIVE TIME: 15 Minutes
TOTAL TIME: 2 Hours

KOURABIEDES

These traditional Greek Christmas treats are powered by the warming flavor of ouzo.

1 cup (227 g) unsalted butter, softened

¾ cup (150 g) sugar

1 teaspoon (5 ml) pure vanilla extract

1 tablespoon (15 ml) ouzo

2 (100 g) eggs

3¼ cups (390 g) all-purpose flour, plus more as needed

1¼ cups (120 g) almond flour

Pinch of table salt

3 tablespoons (45 ml) orange blossom water

1½ cups (170 g) confectioners' sugar

---

1. In the work bowl of a stand mixer fitted with the paddle attachment, cream the butter and sugar on medium speed until the mixture is very light and fluffy, 2 to 3 minutes, scraping down the work bowl as necessary.

2. Add the vanilla, ouzo, eggs, flours, and salt and beat until the mixture comes together as a shaggy dough. Turn the dough out onto a flour-dusted work surface and gently knead it for 30 seconds. Divide the dough half and form each piece into a log. Cover the dough with plastic wrap and chill it in the refrigerator for 1 hour.

3. Preheat the oven to 400°F and line two sheet pans with parchment paper. Cut the dough into 40 pieces, form each one into a small ball, and place them on the pans, making sure to leave 1 inch between them. Place one pan of cookies in the oven at a time. Bake until they are set and golden brown, 13 to 15 minutes, rotating the pans halfway through.

4. Remove the cookies from the oven and transfer them to wire racks. Brush the cookies with the orange blossom water, roll them in the confectioners' sugar, and let them cool completely before enjoying.

KOURABIEDES

page 165

YIELD: 30 Cookies

ACTIVE TIME: 15 Minutes

TOTAL TIME: 3 Hours

CAFÉ COOKIES

It's tough to make a wrong move when the time comes to choose a cookie to enjoy beside a cup of coffee, though it's hard to imagine making a better choice than these cookies.

¼ cup (60 ml) whole milk

2 tablespoons (14 g) instant espresso powder

2 cups (240 g) all-purpose flour, plus more as needed

1 cup (100 g) hazelnuts, coarsely ground

1 (50 g) egg

½ cup (105 g) light brown sugar

1 cup (227 g) unsalted butter, chilled and cubed

Seeds of 1 vanilla bean

1 cup (170 g) chopped gianduja chocolate

---

1. Place the milk and espresso powder in a saucepan and warm the mixture over medium heat, stirring until the espresso powder dissolves. Remove the pan from heat.
2. Place the remaining ingredients, except for the gianduja, in the work bowl of a stand mixer fitted with the paddle attachment and beat to combine. Add the espresso milk and work the mixture until it comes together as a smooth dough. Form the dough into a disk, cover it with plastic wrap, and chill it in the refrigerator for 2 hours.
3. Preheat the oven to 350°F and line two sheet pans with parchment paper. Place the dough on a flour-dusted work surface and roll it out until it is about ⅛ inch thick. Cut the dough into small rounds and arrange them on the pans, making sure to leave 1 inch between them.
4. Place one pan of cookies in the oven at a time. Bake until they are set and golden brown, 12 to 14 minutes, rotating the pans halfway through. Remove the cookies from the oven and let them cool on the pans for a few minutes before transferring them to wire racks to cool completely.
5. Fill a small saucepan halfway with water and bring it to a simmer. Place the gianduja in a heatproof bowl, place it over the simmering water, and stir until the gianduja is melted and smooth. Remove the bowl from heat and briefly let the gianduja cool. Spread it on top of the cookies and let it set before enjoying.

YIELD: 24 Cookies
ACTIVE TIME: 15 Minutes
TOTAL TIME: 1 Hour

PARMESAN & PEPPER SHORTBREAD

These savory shortbreads would work wonderfully at a springtime brunch.

⅔ cup (150 g) unsalted butter, chilled and cubed

1½ cups (180 g) all-purpose flour, plus more as needed

½ cup (50 g) freshly grated Parmesan cheese

2 teaspoons (4 g) freshly ground black pepper

---

1. Preheat the oven to 350°F and line two sheet pans with parchment paper. Combine the butter and flour in a mixing bowl and work the mixture with a pastry cutter until it resembles coarse bread crumbs. Add the Parmesan and black pepper and gently knead the mixture until it comes together as a smooth dough.
2. Place the dough on a flour-dusted work surface and roll it out to about ⅛ inch thick. Cut the dough into rounds and arrange them on the pans, making sure to leave 1 inch between them.
3. Place one pan of cookies in the oven at a time. Bake until they are dry to the touch and golden brown, 12 to 14 minutes, rotating the pans halfway through.
4. Remove the cookies from the oven, transfer them to wire racks, and let them cool completely before enjoying.

YIELD: 24 Cookies
ACTIVE TIME: 45 Minutes
TOTAL TIME: 3 Hours

GORO COOKIES

Part waffle, part cookie, it's easy to see how making these beautiful treats became a holiday tradition in Norway.

---

1. Using a handheld mixer, whip the cream until it holds soft peaks. Set aside.
2. Place the egg white and sugar in the work bowl of a stand mixer fitted with the whisk attachment and whip until the mixture holds soft peaks. Add the whipped cream to the meringue and fold to combine.
3. Place the butter, flour, cardamom, vanilla, and egg yolk in a food processor and pulse to combine. Add the mixture to the meringue mixture, fit the stand mixer with the paddle attachment, and beat until the resulting mixture comes together as a smooth dough. Divide the dough in half, cover each piece with plastic wrap, and chill the dough in the refrigerator for 2 hours.
4. Remove one piece of dough from the refrigerator, place it on a flour-dusted work surface, and roll it into a 1/16-inch-thick rectangle. Cut the sheet to fit a goro iron.
5. Coat the goro iron with nonstick cooking spray and warm it over medium-high heat. Add the dough to the goro iron and cook until the cookies are a light golden brown, 2 to 4 minutes, turning the iron every 20 seconds or so to ensure even cooking.
6. Remove the goro from the iron and cut them into the desired shapes and sizes. Transfer them to a wire rack and let them cool completely.
7. Repeat Steps 3, 4, and 5 with the remaining piece of dough.

10 tablespoons (150 ml) heavy cream

1 (50 g) egg, white and yolk separated

⅗ cup (120 g) sugar

1⅓ cups plus 1 tablespoon (325 g) unsalted butter

1¼ cups (150 g) all-purpose flour, plus more as needed

¼ teaspoon (0.5 g) ground cardamom

½ teaspoon (2.5 ml) pure vanilla extract

1 cup (227 g) unsalted butter, softened

1 cup (210 g) light brown sugar

1 (50 g) egg

2⅘ cups all-purpose flour, plus more as needed

1 teaspoon (4 g) baking powder

½ teaspoon (2.5 g) table salt

1½ cups (255 g) semisweet chocolate chips

½ cup (60 g) chopped walnuts

YIELD: 48 Cookies
ACTIVE TIME: 40 Minutes
TOTAL TIME: 3 Hours

CHOCOLATE & WALNUT SUGAR COOKIES

Sugar cookies always seemed freighted with icing and candies, but cutting against their inherent sweetness with your add-ons is well worth exploring.

---

1. In the work bowl of a stand mixer fitted with the paddle attachment, cream the butter and brown sugar on medium speed until the mixture is very light and fluffy, 2 to 3 minutes, scraping down the work bowl as necessary.
2. Add the egg and beat until incorporated, again scraping the work bowl as necessary. When the egg has been incorporated, scrape down the work bowl, add the flour, baking powder, and salt, and beat until the mixture comes together as a smooth dough. Cover the dough with plastic wrap and chill it in the refrigerator for 2 hours.
3. Preheat the oven to 350°F and line three sheet pans with parchment paper. Place the dough on a flour-dusted work surface and roll it out until it is approximately ¼ inch thick. Use cookie cutters to cut the dough into the desired shapes and place them on the pans, making sure to leave 1 inch between them.
4. Place one pan of cookies in the oven at a time and chill the other cookies in the refrigerator. Bake until their edges are lightly golden brown, 8 to 10 minutes, rotating the pans halfway through. Remove the cookies from the oven, transfer them to a wire rack, and let them cool.
5. Bring water to a simmer in a small saucepan. Place the chocolate chips in a heatproof bowl, place the bowl over the simmering water, and stir the chocolate chips until they have melted. Dip the one end of the cookies into the melted chocolate and sprinkle some walnuts over the chocolate. Let the chocolate set before enjoying.

YIELD: 25 Cookies

ACTIVE TIME: 40 Minutes

TOTAL TIME: 25 Hours

RICCIARELLI

These biscuits from Siena, Tuscany, are believed to have originated in the fourteenth century.

2 (60 g) egg whites

1 teaspoon (5 ml) fresh lemon juice

Seeds of 1 vanilla bean

2 drops of bitter almond extract

Zest of 1 orange

2 cups (200 g) almond flour

1¾ cups (200 g) confectioners' sugar, plus more as needed

---

1. Place the egg whites, lemon juice, vanilla seeds, bitter almond extract, and orange zest in the work bowl of a stand mixer fitted with the paddle attachment and beat until the mixture is foamy.
2. Add the almond flour and confectioners' sugar and beat until the mixture comes together as a soft dough. Form the dough into a ball, cover it with plastic wrap, and chill it in the refrigerator for 24 hours.
3. Preheat the oven to 300°F and line a sheet pan with parchment paper. Generously dust a work surface with confectioners' sugar and place more on a plate. Place the dough on the work surface and shape it into a 1-inch-thick log. Slice it into 1 oz. (30 g) pieces, roll them in the confectioners' sugar until they are completely coated, and form them into ovals or diamonds, flattening and lengthening them.
4. Place the ricciarelli on the pan. Wet your fingers, moisten the cookies, and generously sprinkle more confectioners' sugar over the cookies.
5. Place the cookies in the oven and bake them for 5 minutes. Raise the oven's temperature to 350°F and cook until the cookies start to crack, about 5 minutes.
6. Reduce the oven's temperature to 320°F and cook for another 5 minutes. Remove the ricciarelli from the oven, transfer them to a wire rack, and let them cool completely before enjoying.

YIELD: 20 Cookies
ACTIVE TIME: 15 Minutes
TOTAL TIME: 1 Hour

RASPBERRY BUTTERMILK COOKIES

Addictively tart with a slightly floral character, these cooks are a must in early summer.

1¼ cups (150 g) all-purpose flour, plus more as needed

1½ teaspoons (6 g) baking powder

1 teaspoon (2 g) cinnamon

¼ cup (60 g) unsalted butter

¼ cup (50 g) sugar, plus more to top

½ cup (113 g) buttermilk

¾ cup (90 g) raspberries

---

1. Preheat the oven to 375°F and line two sheet pans with parchment paper. Sift the flour, baking powder, and cinnamon into a mixing bowl, add the butter, and work the mixture with a pastry cutter until it resembles fine bread crumbs. Add the sugar, buttermilk, and raspberries and work the mixture until it just comes together as a dough. Let the dough rest for 5 to 10 minutes.
2. Place the dough on a flour-dusted work surface and roll it out to about ¼ inch thick. Cut the dough into rounds and place them on the pans, making sure to leave 1½ inches between them. Sprinkle additional sugar over the cookies.
3. Place one pan of cookies in the oven at a time. Bake until they are firm and golden brown, 13 to 15 minutes, rotating the pans halfway through.
4. Remove the cookies from the oven, transfer them to a wire rack, and let them cool completely before enjoying.

YIELD: 12 Cookies
ACTIVE TIME: 15 Minutes
TOTAL TIME: 1 Hour and 15 Minutes

THYME & PINK PEPPERCORN SANDWICH COOKIES

The Roquefort supplies a surprising amount of sweetness in what, at first glance, seems to be a wholly savory cookie.

¾ cup (90 g) all-purpose flour, sifted; plus more as needed

¼ cup (60 g) unsalted butter, melted and cooled

1½ teaspoons (2 g) pink peppercorns, crushed

1 teaspoon (1 g) dried thyme

1 tablespoon (3 g) fresh thyme

½ teaspoon (3 g) table salt

1 (12 g) egg yolk

Roquefort Cream (see page 355)

---

1. Place the flour, butter, peppercorns, dried thyme, fresh thyme, and salt in a food processor and pulse until the mixture resembles fine bread crumbs. Add the egg yolk and pulse until the mixture comes together as a smooth dough, adding a little cold water if the dough is struggling to come together. Form the dough into a disk, cover it with plastic wrap, and chill it in the refrigerator for 15 minutes.

2. Preheat the oven to 350°F and line two sheet pans with parchment paper. Place the dough on a flour-dusted work surface and roll it out to about ⅓ inch thick. Cut the dough into small rounds and arrange them on the pans, making sure to leave 1 inch between them.

3. Place one pan of cookies in the oven at a time. Bake until they are golden brown and their edges are set, 10 to 12 minutes, rotating the pans halfway through.

4. Remove the cookies from the oven and let them cool on the pans.

5. Spread the Roquefort Cream over the flat sides of half of the cookies. Assemble the sandwiches with the other cookies and enjoy.

YIELD: 24 Cookies
ACTIVE TIME: 15 Minutes
TOTAL TIME: 2 Hours

TOFFEE & PECAN STARS

You can cut these cookies into any shape you want, but we feel that stars are the most fitting, to hint at the heights they attain.

¾ cup (170 g) unsalted butter, softened

⅓ cup (70 g) sugar

3 tablespoons (40 g) light brown sugar

2 teaspoons (10 ml) pure vanilla extract

1⅔ cups (200 g) all-purpose flour, plus more as needed

6 tablespoons (30 g) cornstarch

¼ teaspoon (1 g) table salt

1 cup (115 g) chopped pecans

1 cup (155 g) toffee pieces

Confectioners' sugar, to dust

---

1. In the work bowl of a stand mixer fitted with the paddle attachment, cream the butter, sugar, brown sugar, and vanilla on medium speed until the mixture is very light and fluffy, 2 to 3 minutes, scraping down the work bowl as necessary.

2. Add the flour, cornstarch, and salt and beat until the mixture comes together as a smooth dough. Add the pecans and toffee and beat until they are evenly distributed. Form the dough into a disk, cover it with plastic wrap, and chill it in the refrigerator for 1 hour.

3. Preheat the oven to 350°F and line two sheet pans with parchment paper. Place the dough on a flour-dusted work surface and roll it out to about ¼ inch thick. Use star-shaped cookie cutters to cut the dough into cookies and place them on the pans, making sure to leave 1 inch between them.

4. Place one pan of cookies in the oven at a time. Bake until their edges are golden brown, 10 to 12 minutes, rotating the pans halfway through.

5. Remove the cookies from the oven and let them cool on the pans for a few minutes. Transfer the cookies to a wire rack and let them cool completely. Dust the cookies with confectioners' sugar before enjoying.

1 cup (227 g) unsalted butter, softened

Zest of 1 lemon

1 cup (200 g) sugar

¾ teaspoon (4 g) pure vanilla extract

2 (100 g) eggs

2⅓ cups (280 g) all-purpose flour

1 teaspoon (4.5 g) baking powder

½ teaspoon (3 g) table salt

1½ cups (170 g) slivered almonds, toasted

YIELD: 24 Biscotti
ACTIVE TIME: 1 Hour
TOTAL TIME: 4 Hours and 30 Minutes

LEMON & ALMOND BISCOTTI

A light biscotti that is as beautiful as it is delicious. Unless you have considerable willpower, make sure you only whip these up when company is coming over.

---

1. Line a sheet pan with parchment paper. In the work bowl of a stand mixer fitted with the paddle attachment, cream the butter, lemon zest, sugar, and vanilla on medium speed until the mixture is very light and fluffy, 2 to 3 minutes, scraping down the work bowl as necessary.
2. Add the eggs one at a time and beat on low until incorporated, again scraping the work bowl as needed. When both eggs have been incorporated, scrape down the work bowl, add the remaining ingredients, reduce the speed to low, and beat until the mixture comes together as a smooth dough.
3. Place the dough on the pan and form it into a log that is the length of the pan and anywhere from 3 to 4 inches wide. Chill the dough in the refrigerator for 1 hour.
4. Preheat the oven to 350°F. Place the biscotti dough in the oven and bake until it is golden brown and a cake tester comes out clean when inserted into the center, 25 to 30 minutes. Remove the biscotti from the oven, transfer it to a wire rack, and let it cool completely before chilling it in the refrigerator for 2 hours.
5. Preheat the oven to 250°F. Cut the biscotti to the desired size, place them on their sides, place them in the oven, and bake for 10 minutes. Remove from the oven, turn them over, and bake until they are crispy and golden brown, 6 to 8 minutes. Remove the biscotti from the oven and let them cool completely before enjoying.

YIELD: 40 Cookies

ACTIVE TIME: 15 Minutes

TOTAL TIME: 1 Hour and 30 Minutes

VANILLA & MATCHA COOKIES

Earthy, sweet, bitter, and umami: a little bit of matcha packs a powerful punch.

1 cup (227 g) unsalted butter, softened

½ cup (100 g) sugar

1 teaspoon (5 ml) pure vanilla extract

2⅔ cups (320 g) all-purpose flour, plus more as needed

2 pinches of table salt

1 tablespoon (2 g) matcha powder

2 cups (227 g) confectioners' sugar

---

1. In the work bowl of a stand mixer fitted with the paddle attachment, cream the butter and sugar on medium speed until the mixture is very light and fluffy, 2 to 3 minutes, scraping down the work bowl as necessary. Add the vanilla and beat to incorporate.

2. Add the flour, salt, and matcha powder and beat until the mixture comes together as a smooth dough. Place dough on a flour-dusted work surface and gently roll it into a log. Cover the dough with plastic wrap and chill it in the refrigerator for 30 minutes.

3. Preheat the oven to 350°F and line two sheet pans with parchment paper. Place the confectioners' sugar in a bowl. Cut the log into ⅓-inch-thick slices, toss them in the confectioners' sugar, and arrange them on the pans, making sure to leave 1 inch between them. Place one pan of cookies in the oven at a time. Bake until their edges are golden brown, 10 to 12 minutes, rotating the pans halfway through.

4. Remove the cookies from the oven and let them cool on the pans for a few minutes. Transfer the cookies to a wire rack and let them cool completely before enjoying.

YIELD: 36 Cookies
ACTIVE TIME: 20 Minutes
TOTAL TIME: 2 Hours

CLASSIC GINGERBREAD COOKIES

Most know it as a Christmas classic, but gingerbread's roots as a foundational piece of celebrations seem to date all the way back to the ancient Greeks and Egyptians, who featured a rudimentary form of the cookie at various ceremonies.

---

1. In the work bowl of a stand mixer fitted with the paddle attachment, cream the butter, brown sugar, and molasses on medium speed until the mixture is very light and fluffy, 2 to 3 minutes, scraping down the work bowl as necessary.
2. Add the egg and beat until it is incorporated, again scraping the work bowl as necessary. When the egg has been incorporated, scrape down the work bowl, add the vanilla, and beat to incorporate. Add the flour, baking soda, ginger, apple pie spice, salt, and pepper and beat until the mixture comes together as a smooth dough.
3. Divide the dough in half and form each piece into a disk. Cover the dough with plastic wrap and chill it in the refrigerator for 1 hour.
4. Preheat the oven to 350°F and line three sheet pans with parchment paper. Place the dough on a flour-dusted work surface and roll it out to about ¼ inch thick. Dip cookie cutters in flour, cut the dough into the desired shapes, and arrange the cookies on the pans, making sure to and place them in the oven.
5. Place one pan of cookies in the oven at a time. Bake until they are firm, 10 to 12 minutes, rotating the pans halfway through.
6. Remove the cookies from the oven and let them cool on the pans for a few minutes. Transfer the cookies to a wire rack and let them cool completely. When the cookies have cooled, decorate them with the icing and candies (if desired).

¾ cup (170 g) unsalted butter, softened

½ cup (105 g) light brown sugar

⅔ cup (225 ml) molasses

1 (50 g) egg, at room temperature

½ teaspoon (2.5 ml) pure vanilla extract

3 cups (360 g) all-purpose flour, plus more as needed

1 teaspoon (4.5 g) baking soda

1 teaspoon (4.5 g) ground ginger

1 teaspoon (2 g) apple pie spice

½ teaspoon (2 g) table salt

¼ teaspoon (1 g) black pepper

Royal Icing (see page 353)

Candies, to decorate (optional)

YIELD: 24 Cookies

ACTIVE TIME: 20 Minutes

TOTAL TIME: 2 Hours and 30 Minutes

SCOTTISH SHORTBREAD

In a book filled with shortbread recipes, this should be considered the standard.

1¼ cups (255 g) unsalted butter

½ cup plus 2 tablespoons (125 g) sugar

3 cups (360 g) all-purpose flour

1 teaspoon (5 g) table salt

---

1. Preheat the oven to 325°F. Grate the butter into a bowl and place it in the freezer for 30 minutes.
2. Place ½ cup of the sugar, the flour, salt, and frozen butter in the work bowl of a stand mixer fitted with the paddle attachment and beat on low speed until the mixture is fine like sand, taking care not to overwork the mixture.
3. Press the mixture into a round, 9-inch tart pan, place it in the oven, and bake until the shortbread is golden brown and dry to the touch, about 1 hour and 15 minutes.
4. Remove the shortbread from the oven and sprinkle the remaining sugar over the top. Let the shortbread cool and cut it into wedges to serve.

YIELD: 20 Cookies

ACTIVE TIME: 20 Minutes

TOTAL TIME: 1 Hour and 30 Minutes

CORTADILLOS DE ANÍS

The lard keys these Spanish Christmas favorites, as it produces an irresistibly rich, crispy cookie.

3 (90 g) egg whites

2 cups (450 g) lard

1 cup plus 1 tablespoon (115 g) sugar

½ cup (113 ml) anise liqueur

Juice of 1 lemon

4⅙ cups (500 g) all-purpose flour, plus more as needed

20 blanched almonds

Confectioners' sugar, to dust

---

1. Preheat the oven to 350°F and line two sheet pans with parchment paper. Place the egg whites in a mixing bowl and beat them with a handheld mixer until they hold soft peaks. Set the egg whites aside.
2. In the work bowl of a stand mixer fitted with the paddle attachment, cream the lard and sugar on medium speed until the mixture is very light and fluffy, 2 to 3 minutes, scraping down the work bowl as necessary.
3. Add the liqueur and lemon juice and beat to incorporate. With the mixer running, gradually add the flour until the mixture comes together as a soft, smooth dough. Add the beaten egg whites and fold to incorporate them.
4. Place the dough on a flour-dusted work surface and roll it into a rectangle. Cut the dough into 20 rectangles, place them on the pans, making sure to leave 1 inch between them, and press an almond into the center of each cookie. Place one pan of cookies in the oven at a time. Bake until they are golden brown, 18 to 20 minutes, rotating the pans halfway through.
5. Remove the cookies from the oven and let them cool on the pans for a few minutes before transferring them to a wire rack. Sprinkle confectioners' sugar over the top and let the cookies cool completely before enjoying.

YIELD: 24 Cookies
ACTIVE TIME: 15 Minutes
TOTAL TIME: 2 Hours

GLUTEN-FREE LAVENDER SHORTBREAD

A bit of lavender infuses a ho-hum shortbread with a flavor that matches the pleasant character of its texture.

¾ cup (170 g) unsalted butter, melted

2 tablespoons (3 g) dried lavender buds

⅓ cup (65 g) sugar

2½ cups (390 g) gluten-free all-purpose flour, plus more as needed

½ teaspoon (2 g) gluten-free baking powder

---

1. Place the butter in the work bowl of a stand mixer fitted with the paddle attachment. Crush the lavender using a mortar and pestle and stir it into the melted butter. Add the sugar, flour, and baking powder and beat the mixture until it comes together as a smooth dough. Form the dough into a disk, cover it with parchment paper, and chill it in the refrigerator for 1 hour.
2. Preheat the oven to 350°F and line two sheet pans with parchment paper. Place the dough on a flour-dusted work surface and roll it out to about ¼ inch thick. Cut it into rounds and arrange them on the pans, making sure to leave 1 inch between them.
3. Place one pan of cookies in the oven at a time. Bake until they are golden brown, 12 to 14 minutes, rotating the pans halfway through.
4. Remove the cookies from the oven and let them cool on the pans for a few minutes. Transfer the cookies to a wire rack and let them cool completely before enjoying.

YIELD: 40 Cookies
ACTIVE TIME: 15 Minutes
TOTAL TIME: 2 Hours

HEIDESAND

Deliciously crumbly and irresistibly light, this traditional German shortbread is among the best in that category.

¾ cup (170 g) unsalted butter, melted

½ cup (100 g) sugar

2½ cups (300 g) all-purpose flour

½ teaspoon (2 g) baking powder

---

1. Place the butter in the work bowl of a stand mixer fitted with the paddle attachment. Add ⅓ cup of the sugar, the flour, and baking powder and beat the mixture until it comes together as a smooth dough. Divide the dough in half and roll it into 1-inch-thick logs.
2. Place the remaining sugar on a plate and roll the dough in it until completely covered. Cover the dough with plastic wrap and chill it in the refrigerator for 1 hour.
3. Preheat the oven to 350°F and line two sheet pans with parchment paper. Cut each log into ½-inch-thick slices and place them on the pans, making sure to leave 1 inch between them. Place one pan of cookies in the oven at a time. Bake until they are golden brown, 10 to 12 minutes, rotating the pans halfway through.
4. Remove the cookies from the oven and let them cool on the pans for a few minutes. Transfer the cookies to wire racks and let them cool completely before enjoying.

½ cup (113 g) unsalted butter, softened

Zest of 1 orange

1 cup (200 g) sugar

¾ teaspoon (4 g) pure vanilla extract

2 (100 g) eggs

2⅓ cups (280 g) all-purpose flour

1 teaspoon (4.5 g) baking powder

½ teaspoon (3 g) table salt

1 cup (120 g) shelled pistachios, toasted

1 cup (115 g) dried cranberries

YIELD: 24 Biscotti
ACTIVE TIME: 1 Hour
TOTAL TIME: 4 Hours and 30 Minutes

CRANBERRY, ORANGE & PISTACHIO BISCOTTI

Feel free to swap in your favorite fruits and nuts for the pistachios and cranberries here.

---

1. Line a sheet pan with parchment paper. In the work bowl of a stand mixer fitted with the paddle attachment, cream the butter, orange zest, sugar, and vanilla on medium speed until the mixture is very light and fluffy, 2 to 3 minutes, scraping down the work bowl as necessary.
2. Add the eggs one at a time and beat on low until incorporated, again scraping the work bowl as needed. When both eggs have been incorporated, scrape down the work bowl, add the remaining ingredients, reduce the speed to low, and beat until the mixture comes together as a smooth dough.
3. Place the dough on the pan and form it into a log that is the length of the pan and anywhere from 3 to 4 inches wide. Chill the dough in the refrigerator for 1 hour.
4. Preheat the oven to 350°F. Place the biscotti dough in the oven and bake until it is golden brown and a cake tester comes out clean when inserted into the center, 25 to 30 minutes. Remove the biscotti from the oven, transfer it to a wire rack, and let it cool completely before chilling it in the refrigerator for 2 hours.
5. Preheat the oven to 250°F. Cut the biscotti to the desired size, place them on their sides, place them in the oven, and bake for 10 minutes. Remove from the oven, turn them over, and bake until they are crispy and golden brown, 6 to 8 minutes. Remove the biscotti from the oven and let them cool completely before enjoying.

YIELD: 48 Cookies
ACTIVE TIME: 1 Hour
TOTAL TIME: 2 Hours

RUGELACH

Raisins and chopped walnuts are another popular filling for this treasured Jewish treat, which lies somewhere in the transcendent space between a cookie and a pastry.

---

1. To begin preparations for the dough, place the butter and cream cheese in the work bowl of a stand mixer fitted with the paddle attachment and beat until the mixture is smooth and fluffy, 2 to 3 minutes, scraping down the work bowl as necessary. Combine the flour and salt in a mixing bowl. With the mixer running on low, gradually add the flour mixture to the cream cheese mixture until the resulting mixture comes together as a smooth dough. Divide the dough into four pieces, cover them with plastic wrap, and chill them in the refrigerator for 1 hour.
2. Preheat the oven to 350°F and line three sheet pans with parchment paper. Place one piece of dough between two sheets of waxed paper and roll it into a 12-inch circle.
3. To begin preparations for the filling, combine sugar and cinnamon in a bowl. Brush the dough with 1 tablespoon of melted butter, sprinkle 3 tablespoons of cinnamon sugar and 2 tablespoons of pecans over the butter, and cut the round into 12 wedges. Starting at the rounded end, roll up the wedges and arrange them on the pans, making sure to leave 2 inches between them. Curve the ends slightly to give the rugelach a crescent shape. Repeat with the remaining pieces of dough and the ingredients for the filling; you will have some melted butter and cinnamon sugar left over.
4. Place one pan of rugelach in the oven at a time. Bake until they are golden brown, about 24 minutes, rotating the pans halfway through.
5. Remove the cookies from the oven and transfer them to wire racks. Brush the warm rugelach with the remaining melted butter, sprinkle the remaining cinnamon sugar over the top, and let the rugelach cool slightly before enjoying.

FOR THE DOUGH

1 cup (227 g) unsalted butter, softened

1 cup (227 g) cream cheese, softened

2 cups (240 g) all-purpose flour

½ teaspoon (2 g) table salt

FOR THE FILLING

1 cup sugar

2 tablespoons cinnamon

½ cup unsalted butter, melted

½ cup finely diced pecans

YIELD: 100 Canestrelli

ACTIVE TIME: 40 Minutes

TOTAL TIME: 2 Hours

CANESTRELLI LIGURI

These cookies from Liguria are famed for their crumbly nature, which is likely due to the presence of hard-boiled egg yolks in the mix.

2⅔ cups (300 g) all-purpose flour, plus more as needed

7 oz. potato starch

1⅓ cups (150 g) confectioners' sugar, plus more to top

Zest of 1 lemon

Seeds of 1 vanilla bean

1 cup plus 6 tablespoons (310 g) unsalted butter, chopped

6 (90 g) hard-boiled egg yolks, crushed

---

1. Place the flour, potato starch, confectioners' sugar, lemon zest, and vanilla seeds in the work bowl of a stand mixer fitted with the paddle attachment and beat on medium speed until well combined.
2. With the mixer running, gradually add the butter and beat to incorporate. Add the egg yolks and beat until the mixture just comes together as a smooth dough. Place the dough on a flour-dusted work surface and flatten it slightly. Cover the dough with plastic wrap and chill it in the refrigerator for 1 hour.
3. Preheat the oven to 350°F and line three sheet pans with parchment paper. Place the dough on a flour-dusted work surface and roll it out into a ⅓-inch-thick round. Using a flower-shaped cookie cutter, cut the dough into cookies and then cut a ⅓-inch hole in the center of each cookie with a ring cutter.
4. Place the canestrelli on the pans, making sure to leave 1 inch between them. Place one pan of cookies in the oven at a time. Bake until they are golden brown, about 15 minutes, rotating the pans halfway through.
5. Remove the canestrelli from the oven, transfer them to wire racks, and let them cool completely. Dust the canestrelli with confectioners' sugar before enjoying.

YIELD: 72 Cookies

ACTIVE TIME: 20 Minutes

TOTAL TIME: 3 Hours

PEPPARKAKOR

Spicy and intriguingly delicate, these cookies are a Scandinavian take on a gingersnap.

2⅔ cups (320 g) all-purpose flour, plus more as needed

1 cup (85 g) almond meal

1 teaspoon (3 g) cinnamon

1 teaspoon (2 g) ground cloves

2 teaspoons (9.5 g) baking soda

1 teaspoon (2 g) ground ginger

1 teaspoon (2 g) cardamom

1 cup (200 g) sugar

¾ cup (160 g) light brown sugar

1 cup (200 g) unsalted butter, chilled and chopped

1 (50 g) egg

Royal Icing (see page 353)

1. Place the flour, almond meal, cinnamon, cloves, baking soda, ginger, cardamom, sugar, and brown sugar in a mixing bowl and stir to combine. Form a well in the center and place the butter around the well. Place the egg in the well and work the mixture with a pastry cutter until it resembles coarse bread crumbs. Knead the mixture with your hands until it is a smooth dough. Shape the dough into a ball, cover it with plastic wrap, and chill it in the refrigerator for 2 hours.

2. Preheat the oven to 375°F and line two sheet pans with parchment paper. Place the dough on a flour-dusted work surface and roll it out to about ⅛ inch thick. Using Christmas-themed cookie cutters, cut the dough into cookies and arrange them on the pans, making sure to leave 1 inch between them.

3. Place one pan of cookies in the oven at a time. Bake until the edges start to brown, 6 to 8 minutes. Remove the cookies from the oven and transfer them to wire racks to cool.

4. When the cookies have cooled, place the icing in a piping bag fitted with a fine tip and decorate the cookies. Let the icing set for 15 minutes before enjoying.

YIELD: 20 Cookies
ACTIVE TIME: 30 Minutes
TOTAL TIME: 3 Hours

CHOCOLATE-COATED CARAMEL DROPS

The beautiful look of these cookies means that making them will be just as enjoyable as eating them.

¼ cup (57 g) unsalted butter, softened

¼ cup (50 g) light brown sugar

1 (15 g) egg yolk

⅔ cup plus 2 teaspoons (85 g) all-purpose flour, plus more as needed

¼ teaspoon (1 g) baking powder

Pinch of table salt

Dulce de Leche (see page 355)

Coating Chocolate (see page 352)

---

1. In the work bowl of a stand mixer fitted with the paddle attachment, cream the butter and brown sugar on medium speed until the mixture is very light and fluffy, 2 to 3 minutes, scraping down the work bowl as necessary.
2. Add the egg yolk and beat until incorporated, again scraping the work bowl as necessary. When the egg yolk has been incorporated, scrape down the work bowl, add the flour, baking powder, and salt, and beat until the mixture comes together as a smooth dough. Cover the dough with plastic wrap and chill it in the refrigerator for 1 hour.
3. Preheat the oven to 350°F and line three sheet pans with parchment paper. Place the dough on a flour-dusted work surface and roll it out until it is approximately ⅓ inch thick. Cut the dough into 2-inch rounds and place them on the pans, making sure to leave 1 inch between them.
4. Place one pan of cookies in the oven at a time. Bake until their edges are lightly golden brown, 8 to 10 minutes, rotating the pans halfway through. Remove the cookies from the oven, transfer them to a wire rack, and let them cool completely.
5. Place the Dulce de Leche in a piping bag fitted with a large fluted tip and pipe it onto the cookies. Spoon the Coating Chocolate over the Dulce de Leche and cookies until they are completely coated. Place the cookies in the refrigerator and chill until the chocolate has hardened before enjoying.

YIELD: 36 Cookies

ACTIVE TIME: 40 Minutes

TOTAL TIME: 2 Hours

KIPFERL BISCUITS

A heavy dusting of confectioners' sugar is the traditional topping for these beautiful, crescent-shaped cookies. Some Caramelized White Chocolate (see page 356) would be another good option.

1½ cups plus 1½ tablespoons (190 g) all-purpose flour, plus more as needed

½ cup (42 g) cocoa powder

½ teaspoon (1 g) instant espresso powder

¼ teaspoon (1 g) table salt

1 cup (227 g) unsalted butter, divided into tablespoons and softened

¾ cup (85 g) confectioners' sugar, sifted, plus more to top

⅔ cup plus 1 tablespoon (70 g) fine almond flour

1 teaspoon (5 ml) pure vanilla extract

---

1. Place all of the ingredients in the work bowl of a stand mixer fitted with the paddle attachment and beat at medium speed until the mixture comes together as a soft, smooth dough. Divide the dough into two pieces, form each piece into a disk, and cover them with plastic wrap. Chill the dough in the refrigerator for 1 hour.

2. Preheat the oven to 350°F and line two sheet pans with parchment paper. Place the dough on a flour-dusted work surface, roll each piece into a ¾-inch-thick log, and cut the logs into 2-inch-long pieces. Roll them with your hands to form them into cylinders, while tapering and curling the ends to create crescent shapes. Place them on the pans, making sure to leave 1 inch between them.

3. Place one pan of cookies in the oven at a time. Bake until they are firm, 13 to 15 minutes, rotating the pans halfway through.

4. Remove the cookies from the oven and transfer them to wire racks to cool completely. When the cookies have cooled, dust them with additional confectioners' sugar and enjoy.

YIELD: 40 Cookies
ACTIVE TIME: 25 Minutes
TOTAL TIME: 1 Hour and 30 Minutes

FAWORKI

These delicate cookies, which are also known as "angel wings," are a holiday tradition in Poland.

3 (150 g) eggs, at room temperature

¼ cup (60 ml) whole milk

¾ cup (150 g) sugar

½ cup (113 g) unsalted butter, softened

1 teaspoon (4.5 g) baking powder

1 teaspoon (5 ml) pure vanilla extract

½ teaspoon (2 g) table salt

½ teaspoon (1 g) freshly grated nutmeg

4 cups plus 2 tablespoons (495 g) all-purpose flour, plus more as needed

Canola oil, as needed

Confectioners' sugar, to dust

---

1. In the work bowl of a stand mixer fitted with the paddle attachment, cream the eggs, milk, sugar, and butter on medium speed until the mixture is very light, 2 to 3 minutes, scraping down the work bowl as necessary. Add the baking powder, vanilla, salt, nutmeg, and flour and beat until the mixture comes together as a soft, smooth dough. Cover the bowl tightly with plastic wrap and chill the dough in the refrigerator for 1 hour.
2. Place the dough on a flour-dusted work surface and roll it out to about ¼ inch thick. Cut the dough into 1-inch-wide strips and then cut the strips on a diagonal every 3 inches to form diamond-shaped cookies.
3. Add canola oil to a Dutch oven until it is 1½ inches deep and warm it to 375°F. Gently slip the cookies into the hot oil a few at a time, using a slotted spoon to turn them as they brown. When cookies are browned all over and crispy, transfer them to a paper towel–lined plate to drain and cool slightly. Sprinkle confectioners' sugar over the cookies and enjoy.

YIELD: 22 Cookies
ACTIVE TIME: 1 Hour
TOTAL TIME: 3 Hours

BACI DI DAMA

"Lady's kisses" in Italian, these sandwich cookies are certain to steal your heart.

---

1. In the work bowl of a stand mixer fitted with the whisk attachment, whip the butter and sugar until the mixture is very fluffy, 2 to 3 minutes, scraping down the work bowl as necessary. Add the egg and whip to incorporate, again scraping down the work bowl as necessary.
2. Add the salt and whip for 2 minutes. Sift the flours into the work bowl and whip until the mixture comes together as a smooth dough.
3. Transfer the dough to a flour-dusted work surface and form it into a log. Cover the dough with plastic wrap and chill it in the refrigerator for 1 hour.
4. Line two sheet pans with parchment paper. Cut the dough into 44 pieces, shape them into small rounds, and arrange them on the pans, making sure to leave 1 inch between them. Chill the baci di dama in the refrigerator for 30 minutes.
5. Preheat the oven to 350°F. Place one pan of cookies in the oven at a time. Bake until they are firm, about 20 minutes, rotating the pans halfway through. Remove the cookies from the oven, transfer them to wire racks, and let them cool.
6. Bring a few inches of water to a simmer in a medium saucepan. Place the gianduja in a heatproof bowl, place it over the simmering water, and stir until the gianduja is melted and smooth. Remove it from heat and let it cool.
7. Transfer the gianduja to a piping bag fitted with a plain tip and pipe some onto half of the cookies. Assemble the baci di dama with the remaining cookies and let the gianduja set before enjoying.

14 tablespoons (200 g) unsalted butter, softened

⅔ cup (135 g) sugar

1 (50 g) egg

Pinch of table salt

2 cups plus 1½ tablespoons (250 g) all-purpose flour, plus more as needed

1¼ cups (110 g) hazelnut flour

⅓ cup (60 g) chopped gianduja chocolate

½ lb. (225 g) dried apricots

½ cup (100 g) sugar

⅔ cup (80 g) all-purpose flour, plus more as needed

¼ teaspoon (1 g) table salt

¼ cup (60 g) cream cheese, softened

½ cup (113 g) unsalted butter, softened

Confectioners' sugar, to dust

YIELD: 32 Cookies
ACTIVE TIME: 30 Minutes
TOTAL TIME: 2 Hours and 30 Minutes

APRICOT SQUARES

You can nestle any fruit in this dough, but none will be lovelier than the sweet and tart apricot.

---

1. Place the apricots in a saucepan and cover them with water. Bring the water to a boil over medium-high heat and cook until the apricots are soft, adding more water to the pan if too much evaporates. Add the sugar and reduce the heat so that the mixture simmers. Cook, stirring to dissolve the sugar, until the liquid thickens into a syrup. Transfer the mixture to a blender or a food processor and puree until it is smooth. Let the mixture cool.
2. Sift the flour and salt into a mixing bowl. In the work bowl of a stand mixer fitted with the paddle attachment, beat the cream cheese and butter on high speed until the mixture is fluffy, 2 to 3 minutes, scraping down the work bowl as needed. With the mixer running on low, gradually add the dry mixture and beat until the resulting mixture comes together as a smooth dough. Divide the dough in half and cover it loosely with plastic wrap. Flatten each piece into a ¾-inch-thick disk and chill the dough in the refrigerator until it is firm, about 2 hours.
3. Preheat the oven to 375°F and line a sheet pan with parchment paper. Place one piece of dough on a flour-dusted work surface and roll it out to about ⅛ inch thick. Cut the dough into as many 1½-inch squares as possible and place approximately 1 teaspoon of the apricot mixture in the center of each square. Gently lift two opposite corners of each square and fold one over the other. Gently press down to seal and transfer the cookie to the pan. Repeat until all of the squares have been filled.
4. Place the cookies in the oven and bake until they are golden brown, 12 to 14 minutes, rotating the pan halfway through. While the cookies are in the oven, repeat Step 3 with the other piece of dough and the remaining filling.
5. Remove the cookies from the oven and place the other pan in the oven. Let the cookies cool briefly on the pans and then transfer them to a wire rack to cool completely.
6. When all of the cookies have been baked and cooled, dust them with confectioners' sugar and enjoy.

YIELD: 36 Cookies
ACTIVE TIME: 1 Hour
TOTAL TIME: 3 Hours

TRADITIONAL ALFAJORES

While other iterations of alfajores have popped up around the globe, this cornstarch-forward version from Spain is the OG.

1 cup plus 2 tablespoons (255 g) unsalted butter, softened

¾ cup (150 g) sugar

½ teaspoon (2 g) table salt

1 tablespoon (15 ml) pure vanilla extract

Zest of 1 lemon

4 (60 g) egg yolks

2½ cups plus 2 tablespoons (300 g) cornstarch

1⅔ cups (200 g) all-purpose flour, plus more as needed

1 teaspoon (4 g) baking powder

1½ cups (480 g) Dulce de Leche (see page 355)

---

1. In the work bowl of a stand mixer fitted with the paddle attachment, cream the butter, sugar, salt, vanilla, and lemon zest on medium speed until the mixture is very light and fluffy, 2 to 3 minutes, scraping down the work bowl as necessary.
2. Add the egg yolks and beat to incorporate, again scraping down the work bowl as necessary. Add the cornstarch, flour, and baking powder, reduce the speed to low, and beat until the mixture comes together as a smooth dough. Form the into a disk, cover it with plastic wrap, and chill it in the refrigerator for 2 hours.
3. Preheat the oven to 350°F and line three sheet pans with parchment paper. Place the dough on a flour-dusted work surface and roll it out to about ¼ inch thick. Cut the dough into 2-inch rounds and place them on the pans, making sure to leave 1 inch between them.
4. Place one pan of cookies in the oven at a time and chill the other cookies in the refrigerator. Bake until they are lightly golden brown at their edges, 8 to 10 minutes, rotating the pans halfway through. Remove the cookies from the oven, transfer them to a wire rack, and let them cool for 10 minutes.
5. Place about a teaspoon of Dulce de Leche on half of the cookies and use the other cookies to assemble the sandwiches, making sure the Dulce de Leche extends all the way to the edge. Enjoy immediately.

YIELD: 40 Cookies

ACTIVE TIME: 30 Minutes

TOTAL TIME: 2 Hours

ARGENTINIAN ALFAJORES

This alfajores iteration is bit more buttery and cakey than the classic, thanks to the reduced amount of cornstarch.

3 (150 g) eggs

2 (30 g) egg yolks

1½ cups (300 g) sugar

2 teaspoons (10 ml) pure vanilla extract

1 cup (227 g) unsalted butter, softened

1 cup (110 g) cornstarch

3½ cups (420 g) all-purpose flour, plus more as needed

1 tablespoon (12 g) baking powder

1½ cups (480 g) Dulce de Leche (see page 355)

1 cup (85 g) unsweetened shredded coconut

---

1. In the work bowl of a stand mixer fitted with the paddle attachment, cream the eggs, egg yolks, sugar, vanilla, and butter on medium speed until the mixture is very light, 2 to 3 minutes, scraping down the work bowl as necessary.
2. Add the cornstarch, flour, and baking powder, reduce the speed to low, and beat until the mixture comes together as a smooth dough. Form the into a disk, cover it with plastic wrap, and chill it in the refrigerator for 2 hours.
3. Preheat the oven to 375°F, line a sheet pan with parchment paper, and coat it with nonstick cooking spray. Divide the dough into four or five pieces and place all but one back in the refrigerator. Place the dough on a flour-dusted work surface and roll it out until it is about ⅛ inch thick. Cut the dough into 2-inch rounds and arrange them on the pan, making sure to leave 1 inch between them.
4. Place the cookies in the oven and bake until they are lightly golden brown at their edges, 8 to 10 minutes, rotating the pans halfway through. Remove the cookies from the oven, transfer them to a wire rack, and let them cool completely. Repeat Steps 3 and 4 with the remaining dough.
5. When the cookies have cooled, place about a teaspoon of Dulce de Leche on half of the cookies and use the other cookies to assemble the sandwiches, making sure the Dulce de Leche extends all the way to the edge. Roll the edges of the cookies in the coconut until they are coated and enjoy.

YIELD: 20 Cookies

ACTIVE TIME: 15 Minutes

TOTAL TIME: 2 Hours and 30 Minutes

½ cup (113 g) unsalted butter, softened

¼ cup (50 g) sugar

½ cup (105 g) light brown sugar

1 (50 g) egg

1½ cups (180 g) all-purpose flour

1 teaspoon (4 g) baking powder

Pinch of table salt

½ cup (115 g) Chocolate Ganache (see page 351), chilled

CHOCOLATE SWIRL COOKIES

Chilling the ganache before adding it to the dough is key here, as it will have the proper texture to keep it from being completely incorporated into the lighter-colored dough.

---

1. In the work bowl of a stand mixer fitted with the paddle attachment, cream the butter, sugar, and brown sugar on medium speed until the mixture is very light and fluffy, 2 to 3 minutes, scraping down the work bowl as necessary.
2. Add the egg and beat until incorporated, again scraping down the work bowl as necessary. Add the flour, baking powder, and salt and beat until the mixture comes together as a smooth dough. With the mixer running on low speed, add the chocolate ganache, swirling it through the dough. Divide the dough in half, form each piece of dough into a log, and cover them with plastic wrap. Let the dough chill in the refrigerator for 1 hour.
3. Preheat the oven to 350°F and line three sheet pans with parchment paper. Cut the logs into ½-inch-thick slices and place them on the pans, making sure to leave 1 inch between them. Place one pan of cookies in the oven at a time. Bake until they are golden brown and their edges are set, 10 to 12 minutes, rotating the pans halfway through.
4. Remove the cookies from the oven, transfer them to wire racks, and let them cool completely before enjoying.

HAVE A BALL

The majority of the recipes in this chapter fall somewhere between the cookies collected in the previous two sections: they are similar to drop cookies in terms of needing to keep the portions of dough to a similar size and the relative ease of handling, while also sharing the more-structured nature of cut-out cookies, a quality that also inclines them toward crispiness. But there are also moments where these cookies forge their own paths, resulting in rich, buttery, and elegant offerings that are among the most memorable in the entire book.

YIELD: 36 Cookies
ACTIVE TIME: 20 Minutes
TOTAL TIME: 1 Hour

POLVORONES

Taking its name from the Spanish word polvo, meaning "powder," these confections are also popularly known as Mexican wedding cookies. But, interestingly, they originated in medieval Arabia and were brought to Spain by the Moors when they took over Andalusia during the eighth century.

1 cup (227 g) unsalted butter, softened

1¾ (scant) cups (200 g) confectioners' sugar

1 cup (115 g) cake flour, plus more as needed

1¼ cups (140 g) self-rising flour

1 cup (140 g) almonds, blanched and minced

½ teaspoon (5 ml) pure vanilla extract

Warm water (110°F), as needed

---

1. Preheat the oven to 350°F and line two sheet pans with parchment paper. In the work bowl of a stand mixer fitted with the paddle attachment, cream the butter and 1¼ cups (140 g) of the confectioners' sugar at medium speed until the mixture is very light and fluffy.

2. Scrape down the work bowl, add the flours, almonds, and vanilla, and beat until the dough is just combined and very stiff. Add a few drops of water, if necessary, to make it pliable.

3. Form 1 to 1½ oz. (30 to 45 g) portions of the dough into balls and place them on the pans, making sure to leave 1 inch between them. Coat the bottom of a measuring cup with nonstick cooking spray and use it to gently press down on each cookie, flattening them slightly.

4. Place one pan of cookies in the oven at a time. Bake until they are light brown, about 10 minutes, rotating the pans halfway through.

5. Remove the cookies from the oven. Place the remaining confectioners' sugar in a bowl and use a spatula to transfer the cookies to the bowl. Roll the cookies in the sugar until they are evenly coated and then transfer them to wire racks. Let them cool completely before enjoying.

YIELD: 24 Cookies
ACTIVE TIME: 25 Minutes
TOTAL TIME: 1 Hour

SNICKERDOODLES

It's well known that the cream of tartar is essential in these classic cookies. But the cinnamon is just as important, so make sure you use a top-quality offering.

1 cup (227 g) unsalted butter, softened

1⅔ cups (330 g) sugar

1 (50 g) egg, at room temperature

2 teaspoons (10 ml) pure vanilla extract

3 cups (360 g) all-purpose flour

2 teaspoons (6 g) cream of tartar

1 teaspoon (4.5 g) baking soda

2½ teaspoons (6.5 g) cinnamon

½ teaspoon (3 g) table salt

---

1. Preheat the oven to 375°F and line two sheet pans with parchment paper. In the work bowl of a stand mixer fitted with the paddle attachment, cream the butter and 1⅓ cups (265 g) sugar on medium speed until the mixture is very light and fluffy, 2 to 3 minutes, scraping down the work bowl as necessary.

2. Add the egg and beat until incorporated, again scraping the work bowl as necessary. When the egg has been incorporated, scrape down the work bowl, add the vanilla, and beat to incorporate. Add the flour, cream of tartar, baking soda, 1½ teaspoons (4 g) of cinnamon, and the salt and beat until the mixture comes together as a smooth, thick dough. Let the dough rest for 5 to 10 minutes.

3. Place the remaining sugar and remaining cinnamon in a mixing bowl and whisk to combine. Form 1 to 1 ½ oz. (30 to 45 g) portions of the dough into balls, roll them in the cinnamon sugar until completely coated, and place them on the pans, making sure to leave 2 inches between them. Place one pan of cookies in the oven at a time. Bake until they are puffy and very soft, about 10 minutes, rotating the pans halfway through.

4. Remove the cookies from the oven, gently press down on them with a silicone spatula to flatten them slightly, and let them cool on the pans for 10 minutes. Transfer the cookies to wire racks and let them cool completely before enjoying.

YIELD: 50 Cookies
ACTIVE TIME: 40 Minutes
TOTAL TIME: 24 Hours

AMARETTI

It's always wise to avoid nibbling on raw cookie dough, but it's imperative to refrain here, as bitter almonds are toxic in their uncooked form.

1¼ cups (175 g) blanched almonds

1⅓ cups (150 g) confectioners' sugar

2 tablespoons (16 g) chopped bitter almonds

2 (60 g) egg whites

1 teaspoon (5 g) baker's ammonia

---

1. Preheat the oven to 390°F. Place the blanched almonds on a sheet pan, place them in the oven, and toast until they are golden brown, about 8 minutes. Remove the toasted almonds from the oven and let them cool.
2. Place the toasted almonds in a food processor, add the confectioners' sugar and bitter almonds, and pulse until the mixture is finely ground, taking care not to overwork the mixture and release the fat in the almonds.
3. Transfer the mixture to the work bowl of a stand mixer fitted with the paddle attachment. Add the egg whites and baker's ammonia and beat until the resulting mixture comes together as a smooth dough, scraping down the work bowl as necessary. Cover the bowl with plastic wrap and chill it in the refrigerator overnight.
4. Preheat the oven to 300°F and line two sheet pans with parchment paper. Working with damp hands, form the mixture into balls the size of a small walnut and place them on the pans, making sure to leave 1 inch between them.
5. Place one pan of cookies in the oven at a time. Bake until they are golden brown and starting to crack, about 20 minutes, rotating the pans halfway through.
6. Remove the amaretti from the oven, transfer them to wire racks, and let them cool completely before enjoying.

4 cups (500 g) unpeeled almonds

4⅙ cups (500 g) all-purpose flour, plus more as needed

1 teaspoon (2 g) unsweetened cocoa powder

1½ teaspoons (5 g) Pisto (see page 356)

1 teaspoon (5 g) baker's ammonia

2½ cups (500 g) sugar

Zest of 1 orange

Zest of 1 clementine

Zest of ½ lemon

⅓ cup (50 g) candied orange peels, minced

Pinch of table salt

3½ tablespoons (50 ml) fresh orange juice

½ cup (113 ml) water

1 (50 g) egg

1 (14 g) egg yolk

Confectioners' sugar, to top

YIELD: 20 Cookies

ACTIVE TIME: 1 Hour

TOTAL TIME: 1 Hour and 30 Minutes

ROCCOCÒ

This Neapolitan cookie has a long history of being celebratory, as it was previously reserved for the holiday season, when people allowed themselves to splurge on then-pricey ingredients.

---

1. Preheat the oven to 350°F. Place the almonds on a sheet pan, place them in the oven, and toast them for 5 minutes. Remove the almonds from the oven and let them cool completely. Leave the oven on.
2. Place the flour, cocoa powder, Pisto, baker's ammonia, sugar, citrus zests, candied orange peels, and salt in the work bowl of a stand mixer fitted with the dough hook.
3. Place the orange juice and water in a measuring cup and warm the mixture to 105°F. With the mixer running on low, gradually add the orange juice mixture to the flour mixture until it has all been incorporated and the resulting mixture comes together as a shaggy dough. Add the almonds and work the dough until they are incorporated. The dough should be dense and not sticky. Work the dough on low speed until it is smooth, about 5 minutes.
4. Divide the dough into three pieces, place them on a flour-dusted work surface, and roll each piece into a log. Tear the logs into pieces that are approximately 3 oz. (90 g) and roll them into thin logs. Line two sheet pans with parchment paper. Form each log into a ring and place them on the pans, making sure to leave 1 inch between them.
5. Place the egg and egg yolk in a bowl and whisk until combined. Brush the rings, inside and out, with the mixture. Place one pan of cookies in the oven at a time. Bake the roccocò until they are golden brown and hard, about 25 minutes, rotating the pans halfway through.
6. Remove the roccocò from the oven and let them cool on the pans for a few minutes before transferring them to wire racks to cool completely. Dust the roccocò with confectioners' sugar before enjoying.

YIELD: 20 Cookies
ACTIVE TIME: 1 Hour
TOTAL TIME: 1 Hour and 30 Minutes

ROCCOCÒ MORBIDI

The classic roccocò on page 231 are hard on the outside and soft inside, which means they are at their best if dipped in sweet wine. Since this use has gradually become less popular, a softer version of roccocò has been developed, featuring honey and more baker's ammonia.

---

1. Preheat the oven to 350°F. Place the almonds on a sheet pan, place them in the oven, and toast them for 5 minutes. Remove the almonds from the oven and let them cool completely. Leave the oven on.
2. Place the flour, cocoa powder, Pisto, baker's ammonia, sugar, zests, honey, candied orange peels, and salt in the work bowl of a stand mixer fitted with the dough hook.
3. Place the orange juice and water in a measuring cup and warm the mixture to 105°F. With the mixer running on low, gradually add the orange juice mixture to the flour mixture until it has all been incorporated and the mixture comes together as a dough.
4. Add the almonds and work the dough until they are incorporated. The dough should be dense and not sticky. Work the dough on low until it is smooth, about 5 minutes. Divide the dough into three pieces, place them on a flour-dusted work surface, and roll each piece into a log. Tear the logs into pieces that are approximately 3 oz. and roll them into thin logs.
5. Line two sheet pans with parchment paper. Form each log into a ring and place them on the pans, making sure to leave 1 inch between them. Place the egg and egg yolk in a bowl and whisk until combined. Brush the rings, inside and out, with the egg wash.
6. Place one pan of cookies in the oven at a time. Bake until the roccocò are golden brown and hard, about 25 minutes.
7. Remove the roccocò from the oven and let them cool on the pans for a few minutes. Transfer them to wire racks and let them cool completely before enjoying.

4 cups (500 g) unpeeled almonds

4⅙ cups (500 g) all-purpose flour, plus more as needed

1 teaspoon (2 g) unsweetened cocoa powder

1½ teaspoons (5 g) Pisto (see page 356)

2 teaspoons (10 g) baker's ammonia

2½ cups (500 g) sugar

Zest of 1 orange

Zest of 1 clementine

Zest of ½ lemon

1 tablespoon plus 1 teaspoon (28 ml) honey

⅓ cup (50 g) candied orange peels, minced

Pinch of table salt

3½ tablespoons (50 ml) fresh orange juice

½ cup (113 ml) water

1 (50 g) egg

1 (14 g) egg yolk

YIELD: 36 Cookies
ACTIVE TIME: 15 Minutes
TOTAL TIME: 1 Hour

PEANUT BUTTER BLOSSOMS

The combination of textures in these cookies is what has catapulted them to classic status.

36 milk chocolate kisses

½ cup (113 g) unsalted butter, softened

½ cup (125 g) creamy peanut butter

½ cup (100 g) sugar, plus more to coat

½ cup (105 g) light brown sugar

1 (50 g) egg

1 teaspoon (5 ml) pure vanilla extract

1⅔ cups (205 g) all-purpose flour

1 teaspoon (4.5 g) baking soda

½ teaspoon (2 g) table salt

---

1. Preheat oven to 375°F. Remove the foil wrap from the chocolate kisses and set them aside. In the work bowl of a stand mixer fitted with the paddle attachment, beat the butter and peanut butter on medium speed until the mixture is fluffy, about 2 minutes. Add the sugars, egg, and vanilla and beat until the mixture is light and fluffy, 2 to 3 minutes, scraping down the work bowl as necessary. Add the flour, baking soda, and salt and beat until the resulting mixture comes together as a smooth dough. Let the dough rest for 5 to 10 minutes.

2. Form tablespoons of the dough into balls, roll them in a bowl of sugar until they are completely coated, and place them on unlined, ungreased sheet pans, making sure to leave 1 inch between them. Place one pan of cookies in the oven at a time. Bake until they are light brown, 8 to 10 minutes, rotating the pans halfway through.

3. Remove the cookies from the oven, top each one with a chocolate kiss, and press down gently. The cookie will crack around the edges, which is precisely what you want. Transfer the cookies to a wire rack and let them cool completely before enjoying.

YIELD: 30 Cookies

ACTIVE TIME: 20 Minutes

TOTAL TIME: 1 Hour and 30 Minutes

GINGER MOLASSES CROSSES

By substituting some aquafaba for the eggs, you can pretty easily transform these cookies into vegan-friendly treats.

6 tablespoons (90 g) margarine

1 cup plus 2 tablespoons (220 g) sugar, plus more to coat

1 (scant) cup (190 g) light brown sugar

2 (100 g) eggs

3 (heaping) tablespoons (70 ml) molasses

2¾ cups (330 g) all-purpose flour

2 teaspoons (9 g) baking soda

½ teaspoon (2 g) table salt

1 teaspoon (2 g) ground ginger

1 teaspoon (2.5 g) cinnamon

---

1. Line two sheet pans with parchment paper. In the work bowl of a stand mixer fitted with the paddle attachment, cream the margarine, sugar, and brown sugar on medium speed until the mixture is light and fluffy, 2 to 3 minutes, scraping down the work bowl as necessary.

2. Add the eggs one at a time and beat until incorporated, again scraping the work bowl as needed. When both eggs have been incorporated, scrape down the work bowl, add the molasses, and beat to incorporate. Place the remaining ingredients in a mixing bowl and whisk to combine. With the mixer running on low, gradually add the dry mixture to the wet mixture and beat until the resulting mixture comes together as a smooth dough. Let the dough rest for 5 to 10 minutes.

3. Place some sugar in a shallow bowl. Form 2-teaspoon portions of the dough into balls and roll them in the sugar. Place the cookies on the pans, making sure to leave 1 inch between them. Using a fork, press down on the cookies, flattening them slightly and making a cross in their tops. Chill the cookies in the refrigerator for 15 minutes.

4. Preheat the oven to 325°F. Place one pan of cookies in the oven at a time. Bake until they are brown and their edges are set, 12 to 14 minutes, rotating the pans halfway through.

5. Remove the cookies from the oven and let them cool on the pans for a few minutes. Transfer the cookies to wire racks and let them cool completely before enjoying.

YIELD: 24 Cookies

ACTIVE TIME: 15 Minutes

TOTAL TIME: 1 Hour

ADDIS ABABA COOKIES

The teff flour supplies these cookies with a lovely, wholesome taste.

- 1½ cups (200 g) teff flour
- ½ teaspoon (2.5 g) table salt
- ¼ teaspoon (1 g) cinnamon
- ½ cup (113 g) unsalted butter, softened
- ½ cup (130 g) creamy almond butter
- ½ cup (150 ml) real maple syrup
- ½ cup (113 g) coconut oil, melted
- 1 teaspoon (5 ml) pure vanilla extract
- ½ cup (65 g) shelled pistachios, chopped
- 2 tablespoons (14 g) brown flaxseeds
- Chocolate Ganache (see page 351), warm

1. Preheat the oven to 350°F and line two sheet pans with parchment paper. In a mixing bowl, combine the teff flour, salt, and cinnamon. Add the butter, almond butter, maple syrup, coconut oil, and vanilla and stir until the mixture comes together as a dough. Add the pistachios and flaxseeds and fold until they are evenly distributed. Let the dough rest for 5 to 10 minutes.
2. Form heaping tablespoons of the dough into balls and arrange them on the pans, making sure to leave 2 inches between them. Coat the bottom of a measuring cup with nonstick cooking spray and use it to gently press down on each cookie, flattening them.
3. Place one pan of cookies in the oven at a time. Bake until their edges are set, 10 to 12 minutes, rotating the pans halfway through.
4. Remove the cookies from the oven and let them cool on the pans for a few minutes. Transfer the cookies to wire racks and let them cool completely.
5. When the cookies have cooled, drizzle the ganache over the top. Let it set before enjoying.

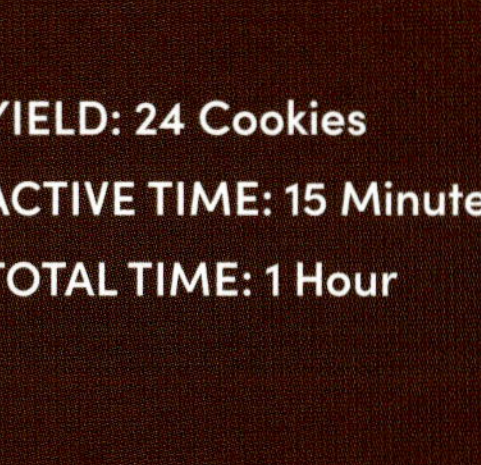

YIELD: 24 Cookies
ACTIVE TIME: 15 Minutes
TOTAL TIME: 1 Hour

BUTTER PECAN COOKIES

Thanks to the decadent pecan, these cookies don't need many ingredients to feel indulgent.

---

2 cups (240 g) all-purpose flour

1½ cups (160 g) pecans, chopped

¼ cup (50 g) sugar

1 cup (227 g) unsalted butter, softened

1 teaspoon (5 ml) pure vanilla extract

---

1. Preheat the oven to 325°F. In the work bowl of a stand mixer fitted with the paddle attachment, combine all of the ingredients and beat on low speed until the mixture comes together as a soft dough, scraping down the work bowl as necessary.
2. Form 1 oz. (30 g) portions of the dough into balls and arrange them on unlined sheet pans, making sure to leave 2 inches between them. Place one pan of cookies in the oven at a time. Bake until they are light golden brown, 10 to 12 minutes, rotating the pans halfway through.
3. Remove the cookies from the oven and let them cool on the pans for a few minutes. Transfer the cookies to a wire rack and let them cool completely before enjoying.

YIELD: 36 Cookies

ACTIVE TIME: 25 Minutes

TOTAL TIME: 45 Minutes

CHOCOLATE-COVERED CHERRY COOKIES

To take these cookies up another level, consider using the maraschino cherries produced by Luxardo.

½ cup (113 g) unsalted butter, softened

1 cup (200 g) sugar

1 (50 g) egg

1½ teaspoons (7.5 ml) pure vanilla extract

1¼ cups (150 g) all-purpose flour

¾ cup (60 g) unsweetened cocoa powder

Pinch of table salt

1 teaspoon (4 g) baking powder

36 maraschino cherries, stems removed, patted dry

1 cup (170 g) semisweet chocolate chips

½ cup (113 ml) sweetened condensed milk

1 tablespoon (15 ml) syrup from jar of maraschino cherries

---

1. Preheat the oven to 350°F and line two sheet pans with parchment paper. In the work bowl of a stand mixer fitted with the paddle attachment, cream the butter and sugar on medium speed until the mixture is very light and fluffy, 2 to 3 minutes, scraping down the work bowl as necessary.

2. Add the egg and vanilla and beat to incorporate, again scraping the work bowl as necessary. Add the flour, cocoa powder, salt, and baking powder and beat until the mixture comes together as a smooth dough.

3. Form tablespoons of the dough into balls and arrange them on the pans, making sure to leave 1 inch between them. Gently push one cherry halfway into each cookie.

4. Place one pan of cookies in the oven at a time. Bake until their edges are set, about 10 minutes, rotating the pans halfway through. Remove the cookies from the oven and let them cool on the pans for a few minutes before transferring them to a wire rack to cool completely.

5. Fill a small saucepan halfway with water and bring it to a gentle simmer. Place the chocolate chips and condensed milk in a heatproof bowl, place it over the simmering water, and stir until the chocolate has melted and the mixture is smooth. Remove the mixture from heat and let it cool for 5 minutes. Stir in the cherry juice and spoon the mixture over the cookies. Let the chocolate set before enjoying.

YIELD: 48 Cookies
ACTIVE TIME: 30 Minutes
TOTAL TIME: 2 Hours

PFEFFERNÜSSE

Spicy and enriched by molasses, these are a great option to bring to a holiday cookie swap.

½ cup (113 g) unsalted butter, softened

1 cup (210 g) light brown sugar

3 tablespoons (60 ml) molasses, warmed

1 (50 g) egg

2⅘ cups (340 g) all-purpose flour

½ teaspoon (3 g) table salt

½ teaspoon (1 g) black pepper

½ teaspoon (1 g) cinnamon

¼ teaspoon (1 g) baking soda

¼ teaspoon (0.5 g) allspice

¼ teaspoon (0.5 g) freshly grated nutmeg

Pinch of ground cloves

2 cups (227 g) confectioners' sugar

---

1. In the work bowl of a stand mixer fitted with the paddle attachment, cream the butter, brown sugar, and molasses on medium speed until the mixture is very light and fluffy, 2 to 3 minutes, scraping down the work bowl as necessary.
2. Add the egg and beat until incorporated, again scraping the work bowl as necessary. When the egg has been incorporated, scrape down the work bowl, add the flour, salt, pepper, cinnamon, baking soda, allspice, nutmeg, and cloves, and beat until the mixture comes together as a smooth dough. Cover the bowl with plastic wrap and chill it in the refrigerator for 1 hour.
3. Preheat the oven to 350°F and line two sheet pans with parchment paper. Form 1 to 1½ oz. (30 to 45 g) portions of the dough into balls and place them on the pans, making sure to leave 1 inch between them. Place one pan of cookies in the oven at a time. Bake until they are firm, 12 to 14 minutes, rotating the pans halfway through.
4. Remove the cookies from the oven and transfer them to wire racks. Let them cool briefly.
5. Place the confectioners' sugar in a bowl and toss the warm cookies in it until they are completely coated. Place the cookies back on the wire racks and let them cool completely before enjoying.

PFEFFERNÜSSE

page 243

YIELD: 24 Cookies
ACTIVE TIME: 15 Minutes
TOTAL TIME: 1 Hour

CHOCOLATE POLVORONES

The famed powdery cookie works just as well when charged by chocolate.

- ⅓ cup (40 g) ground almonds
- 1⅔ cups (190 g) confectioners' sugar
- 1½ cups (180 g) all-purpose flour
- ¾ cup (60 g) unsweetened cocoa powder
- ¼ teaspoon (1.5 g) table salt
- 1 cup (227 g) unsalted butter, cold and cubed
- 1 (50 g) egg

---

1. Preheat the oven to 350°F and line two sheet pans with parchment paper. In a mixing bowl, combine the almonds and ⅔ cup (75 g) confectioners' sugar, then set aside. Sift the flour, cocoa powder, and salt into a separate mixing bowl. Add the butter and work the mixture with a pastry cutter until it comes together as a coarse, crumbly dough. Add the almond mixture to the dough and knead to incorporate. Add the egg and knead until the dough is smooth. Let the dough rest for 5 to 10 minutes.
2. Form 1 to 1½ oz. (30 to 45 g) portions of the dough into balls and place them on the pans, making sure to leave 1 inch between them. Coat the bottom of a measuring cup with nonstick cooking spray and use it to gently press down on each cookie, flattening them slightly.
3. Place one pan of cookies in the oven at a time. Bake until they are firm, 12 to 14 minutes, rotating the pans halfway through.
4. Remove the cookies from the oven and transfer them to a wire rack. Sift the remaining confectioners' sugar over the cookies. Let them cool completely before enjoying.

YIELD: 24 Cookies
ACTIVE TIME: 20 Minutes
TOTAL TIME: 2 Hours

CHOCOLATE TURTLE COOKIES

Just one of these rich treats is enough to satisfy—even for the biggest sweet tooth out there.

- ½ cup (113 g) unsalted butter, softened
- 14 tablespoons (175 g) sugar
- 1 (14 g) egg yolk
- 2 tablespoons (30 ml) whole milk
- 1 teaspoon (5 ml) pure vanilla extract
- 1 cup (120 g) all-purpose flour
- ⅔ cup (55 g) unsweetened cocoa powder
- Pinch of table salt
- 1 (30 g) egg white
- 1 cup (105 g) pecans, minced
- Caramel Sauce (see page 354)

---

1. Preheat the oven to 350°F and line two sheet pans with parchment paper. In the work bowl of a stand mixer fitted with the paddle attachment, cream the butter and sugar on medium speed until the mixture is very light and fluffy, 2 to 3 minutes, scraping down the work bowl as necessary.
2. Add the egg yolk, milk, and vanilla and beat to incorporate, again scraping down the work bowl as necessary. Add the flour, cocoa powder, and salt and beat until the mixture comes together as a smooth dough. Let the dough rest for 5 to 10 minutes.
3. Place the egg white in a bowl and whisk until it is frothy. Place the pecans in a shallow dish. Form tablespoons of the dough into balls, dip the balls in the egg white until completely coated, and roll them in the pecans. Arrange the cookies on the pans, making sure to leave 1 inch between them, and make a small indentation in the centers of the cookies.
4. Place one pan of cookies in the oven at a time. Bake until their edges are set, 10 to 12 minutes, rotating the pans halfway through.
5. Remove the cookies from the oven and let them cool on the pans for a few minutes before transferring them to a wire rack to cool completely.
6. Fill the indentation with some of the caramel, drizzle a little more over the cookies, and let the caramel set before enjoying.

YIELD: 24 Cookies

ACTIVE TIME: 15 Minutes

TOTAL TIME: 2 Hours

¾ cup (170 g) unsalted butter, softened

⅓ cup (40 g) confectioners' sugar

½ cup (100 g) sugar

1 (50 g) egg

1 teaspoon (5 ml) pure vanilla extract

1¾ cups (210 g) all-purpose flour

½ teaspoon (2 g) baking powder

½ teaspoon (3 g) table salt

½ cup (85 g) butterscotch chips

½ cup (85 g) chopped white chocolate

BUTTERSCOTCH & WHITE CHOCOLATE COOKIES

Those who like their cookies on the sweeter side will find no better choice in this book.

---

1. In the work bowl of a stand mixer fitted with the paddle attachment, cream the butter, confectioners' sugar, and sugar on medium speed until the mixture is very light and fluffy, 2 to 3 minutes, scraping down the work bowl as necessary.
2. Add the egg and beat until incorporated, again scraping the work bowl as necessary. When the egg has been incorporated, scrape down the work bowl, add the vanilla, and beat to incorporate. Add the flour, baking powder, and salt and beat until the mixture comes together as a smooth dough. Add the butterscotch chips and white chocolate and beat until they are evenly distributed. Let the dough rest for 5 to 10 minutes.
3. Preheat the oven to 350°F and line two sheet pans with parchment paper. Form 1 to 1½ oz. (30 to 45 g) portions of the dough into balls and place them on the pans, making sure to leave 2 inches between them. Place one pan of cookies in the oven at a time. Bake until they are golden brown, 10 to 12 minutes, rotating the pans halfway through.
4. Remove the cookies from the oven and let them cool on the pans for a few minutes. Transfer the cookies to wire racks and let them cool completely before enjoying.

YIELD: 24 Cookies
ACTIVE TIME: 40 Minutes
TOTAL TIME: 2 Hours

FRUITCAKE COOKIES

The divisive holiday treat will cause no such rancor when translated into cookie form.

3 tablespoons (35 g) currants

Zest of 3 oranges

3 tablespoons (35 g) raisins

2 teaspoons (10 ml) brandy

7 tablespoons (100 g) unsalted butter, softened

⅓ cup (70 g) light brown sugar

½ teaspoon (5 ml) pure vanilla extract

2 teaspoons (14 ml) molasses

1 teaspoon (2 g) pumpkin pie spice

¼ cup (35 g) sliced almonds, chopped

1⅓ cups (150 g) self-rising flour

¼ cup (20 g) almond meal

Royal Icing (optional; see page 353)

---

1. Place the currants, one-third of the orange zest, raisins, and brandy in a bowl, stir to combine, and cover the bowl with plastic wrap. Let the mixture sit for 1 hour.
2. Place the mixture in a food processor and puree until smooth. Preheat the oven to 350°F and line two sheet pans with parchment paper. In the work bowl of a stand mixer fitted with the paddle attachment, cream the butter and brown sugar on medium speed until the mixture is very light and fluffy, 2 to 3 minutes, scraping down the work bowl as necessary. Add the remaining orange zest, vanilla, molasses, and brandy mixture and beat to incorporate, again scraping down the work bowl as necessary. Add the pumpkin pie spice, almonds, flour, and almond meal and work the mixture until it comes together as a smooth dough.
3. Form tablespoons of the dough into balls and arrange them on the pans, making sure to leave 1 inch between them. Place one pan of cookies in the oven at a time. Bake until their edges are set and a cake tester inserted into their centers comes out clean, 12 to 14 minutes, rotating the pans halfway through.
4. Remove the cookies from the oven and let them cool on the pans for a few minutes. Transfer the cookies to a wire rack and let them cool completely. If desired, drizzle the icing over the cookies and let it set before enjoying.

YIELD: 12 Cookies
ACTIVE TIME: 15 Minutes
TOTAL TIME: 1 Hour

MANTECADOS

This crumbly Spanish shortbread is sure to win you over—especially when paired with a hot cup of coffee.

½ cup (113 g) unsalted butter, softened

¼ cup (50 ml) Spanish extra-virgin olive oil

½ cup (100 g) sugar

Zest of ½ lemon

1 teaspoon (5 ml) fresh lemon juice

1 (50 g) egg

1 cup (120 g) all-purpose flour, plus more as needed

¼ teaspoon (1 g) baking powder

---

1. Line a sheet pan with parchment paper. In the work bowl of a stand mixer fitted with the paddle attachment, cream the butter and olive oil until the mixture is light and fluffy. Add the sugar, lemon zest, and lemon juice and beat until the mixture pale and creamy, 2 to 3 minutes, scraping down the work bowl as necessary.
2. Add the egg and beat until incorporated, again scraping the work bowl as necessary. When the egg has been incorporated, scrape down the work bowl, add the flour and baking powder and beat until the mixture comes together as a smooth dough. Let the dough rest for 5 to 10 minutes.
3. Form the dough into 12 balls and place them on the pan, making sure to leave about 2 inches between them. Coat the bottom of a measuring cup with nonstick cooking spray and use it to gently press down on each cookie, flattening them. Chill the cookies in the refrigerator for 15 minutes.
4. Preheat the oven to 375°F. Place the cookies in the oven and bake until they are a light golden brown, 15 to 20 minutes, rotating the pan halfway through.
5. Remove the cookies from the oven and let them cool on the pan for a few minutes. Transfer them to wire racks and let them cool completely before enjoying.

MANTECADOS

page 253

YIELD: 24 Cookies
ACTIVE TIME: 15 Minutes
TOTAL TIME: 1 Hour

LEMON & POPPY SEED COOKIES

To the surprise of no one, one of the baking world's great flavor combinations does not disappoint as a cookie. Consider soaking the poppy seeds in water for a few seconds before adding them to the dough—it's not necessary, but it will make them just a bit more toothsome.

⅔ cup (150 g) unsalted butter, softened

1 cup (200 g) sugar

1 (50 g) egg

1 tablespoon (15 ml) fresh lemon juice

1¾ cups (210 g) all-purpose flour

1 teaspoon (4.5 g) baking powder

2 tablespoons (20 g) poppy seeds

1 tablespoon (6 g) lemon zest

---

1. Preheat the oven to 350°F and line two sheet pans with parchment paper. In the work bowl of a stand mixer fitted with the paddle attachment, cream the butter and sugar on medium speed until the mixture is very light and fluffy, 2 to 3 minutes, scraping down the work bowl as necessary.
2. Add the egg and lemon juice and beat to incorporate, again scraping the work bowl as necessary. Add the flour and baking powder and beat until the mixture comes together as a smooth dough. Add the poppy seeds and lemon zest and beat until they are evenly distributed.
3. Form tablespoons of the dough into balls and arrange them on the pans, making sure to leave 1 inch between them. Place one pan of cookies in the oven at a time. Bake until their edges are a light golden brown, 8 to 10 minutes, rotating the pans halfway through.
4. Remove the cookies from the oven and let them cool on the pans for a few minutes. Transfer the cookies to a wire rack and let them cool completely before enjoying.

YIELD: 18 Cookies

ACTIVE TIME: 15 Minutes

TOTAL TIME: 1 Hour

M&M COOKIES

Your favorite variety of M&Ms will work in these cookies, but we find that the originals work the best.

⅔ cup (150 g) unsalted butter, softened

⅔ cup (70 g) light brown sugar

1 (50 g) egg

1¾ cups (210 g) all-purpose flour

½ teaspoon (2 g) baking soda

Pinch of table salt

1½ cups (255 g) M&Ms

---

1. Preheat the oven to 350°F and line two sheet pans with parchment paper. In the work bowl of a stand mixer fitted with the paddle attachment, cream the butter and brown sugar on medium speed until the mixture is very light and fluffy, 2 to 3 minutes, scraping down the work bowl as necessary.
2. Add the egg and beat to incorporate, again scraping the work bowl as necessary. Add the flour, baking soda, and salt and beat until the mixture comes together as a smooth dough. Add the M&Ms and beat until they are evenly distributed. Let the dough rest for 5 to 10 minutes.
3. Form 2 oz. (60 g) portions of the dough into balls and arrange them on the pans, making sure to leave 2 inches between them. Place one pan of cookies in the oven at a time. Bake until they are golden brown and slightly firm, 12 to 14 minutes, rotating the pans halfway through.
4. Remove the cookies from the oven, transfer them to wire racks, and let them cool completely before enjoying.

YIELD: 24 Cookies
ACTIVE TIME: 15 Minutes
TOTAL TIME: 2 Hours

MATCHA & SESAME SEED COOKIES

The nuttiness supplied by the sesame seeds is a beautiful counter to the earthy matcha.

1 cup (227 g) unsalted butter, softened

1½ tablespoons (9 g) matcha powder

¾ cup (150 g) sugar

1 (50 g) egg

1 teaspoon (5 ml) pure vanilla extract

2¼ cups (250 g) all-purpose flour, plus more as needed

¼ teaspoon (1 g) table salt

2 tablespoons (20 g) black sesame seeds

---

1. Preheat the oven to 350°F and line two sheet pans with parchment paper. In the work bowl of a stand mixer fitted with the paddle attachment, cream the butter, matcha powder, and sugar on medium speed until the mixture is very light and fluffy, 2 to 3 minutes, scraping down the work bowl as necessary.
2. Add the egg and vanilla and beat to incorporate, again scraping the work bowl as necessary. Add the flour and salt and beat until the mixture comes together as a smooth dough. Let the dough rest for 5 to 10 minutes.
3. Form 1½ to 2 oz. (45 to 60 g) portions of the dough into balls and arrange them on the pans, making sure to leave 2 inches between them. Gently press a few sesame seeds onto the top of each cookie. Place one pan of cookies in the oven at a time. Bake until they are slightly firm, 12 to 14 minutes, rotating the pans halfway through.
4. Remove the cookies from the oven, transfer them to wire racks, and let them cool completely before enjoying.

YIELD: 36 Cookies

ACTIVE TIME: 15 Minutes

TOTAL TIME: 1 Hour

ESPRESSO & GIANDUJA BLOSSOMS

As coffee connoisseurs are well aware, the richness of hazelnut and slightly bitter bite of espresso are a willing combination.

½ cup (113 g) unsalted butter, softened

½ cup (100 g) sugar, plus more to coat

½ cup (105 g) light brown sugar

1 (50 g) egg

1 teaspoon (5 ml) pure vanilla extract

1 cup (120 g) all-purpose flour

½ cup (45 g) hazelnut flour

2 tablespoons (14 g) espresso powder

1 teaspoon (4.5 g) baking soda

½ teaspoon (2 g) table salt

Gianduja Crèmeux (see page 358)

---

1. Preheat oven to 375°F and line two sheet pans with parchment paper. In the work bowl of a stand mixer fitted with the paddle attachment, cream the butter, sugar, and brown sugar on medium speed until the mixture is very light and fluffy, 2 to 3 minutes, scraping down the work bowl as necessary.
2. Add the egg and vanilla and beat to incorporate, again scraping the work bowl as necessary. Add the flours, espresso powder, baking soda, and salt and beat until the resulting mixture comes together as a smooth dough. Let the dough rest for 5 to 10 minutes.
3. Form tablespoons of the dough into balls and place them on unlined, ungreased sheet pans, making sure to leave 1 inch between them. Gently press down on the center of each ball to make an indentation. Place one pan of cookies in the oven at a time. Bake until they are light brown, 8 to 10 minutes, rotating the pans halfway through.
4. Remove the cookies from the oven and let them cool on the pans for a few minutes. Transfer the cookies to a wire rack and let them cool completely.
5. When the cookies have cooled, pipe the Gianduja Crèmeux into the indentations and enjoy.

YIELD: 16 Cookies
ACTIVE TIME: 20 Minutes
TOTAL TIME: 1 Hour

OATMEAL RAISIN COOKIES

This classic reached its vaunted status by being more than the sum of its parts.

¼ cup (57 g) unsalted butter, softened

¼ teaspoon (1 g) cinnamon

¾ cup (160 g) light brown sugar

½ cup (100 g) sugar

½ cup (100 ml) extra-virgin olive oil

1 (50 g) egg

1 (15 g) egg yolk

1 teaspoon (5 ml) pure vanilla extract

1 cup (120 g) all-purpose flour

½ teaspoon (2 g) baking soda

¾ teaspoon (3.5 g) table salt

3 cups (340 g) rolled oats

½ cup (80 g) raisins

---

1. Preheat the oven to 350°F and line two sheet pans with parchment paper. In the work bowl of a stand mixer fitted with the paddle attachment, cream the butter, cinnamon, brown sugar, and sugar on medium speed until the mixture is very light and fluffy, 2 to 3 minutes, scraping down the work bowl as necessary.

2. Add the olive oil, egg, egg yolk, and vanilla and beat to incorporate, again scraping the work bowl as necessary. Add the flour, baking soda, and salt and beat until the mixture comes together as a smooth dough. Add the oats and raisins and beat until they are evenly distributed. Let the dough rest for 5 to 10 minutes.

3. Form 1½ to 2 oz. (45 to 60 g) portions of the dough into balls and arrange them on the pans, making sure to leave 2 inches between them. Coat the bottom of a measuring cup with nonstick cooking spray and use it to gently press down on each cookie, flattening them slightly. Place one pan of cookies in the oven at a time. Bake until they are golden brown, 12 to 14 minutes, rotating the pans halfway through.

4. Remove the cookies from the oven and let them cool on the pans for a few minutes. Transfer the cookies to wire racks and let them cool completely before enjoying.

YIELD: 12 Cookies

ACTIVE TIME: 15 Minutes

TOTAL TIME: 1 Hour

ROMANIAN WALNUT & RUM COOKIES

The walnut-shaped molds are not necessary here, but they do make these cookies a bit more visually appealing. If you do not have these molds, simply flatten one side of the balls with a measuring cup before placing them on the sheet pans.

---

1. Preheat the oven to 350°F and line two sheet pans with parchment paper. To begin preparations for the cookies, place the butter and sugar in the work bowl of a stand mixer fitted with the paddle attachment and cream on medium speed until the mixture is very light and fluffy, 2 to 3 minutes, scraping down the work bowl as necessary.
2. Add the egg yolks, vanilla, and milk and beat to incorporate, again scraping the work bowl as necessary. Fit the mixer with the dough hook, add the flour, baking powder, and salt and work the mixture until it comes together as a smooth dough. Let the dough rest for 5 to 10 minutes.
3. Coat walnut-shaped molds with nonstick cooking spray. Form 2 oz. (60 g) portions of the dough into balls and press them into the molds. Remove the cookies from the molds and arrange them, flat side down, on the pans, making sure to leave 1 inch between them. Place one pan of cookies in the oven at a time. Bake until they are golden brown, 12 to 14 minutes, rotating the pans halfway through.
4. Remove the cookies from the oven and let them cool on the pans for a few minutes. Transfer the cookies to wire racks and let them cool completely.
5. While the cookies are cooling, prepare the filling. Place the walnut pieces in a food processor and pulse until they are finely ground. Add the remaining ingredients and blitz until the mixture is smooth, scraping down the work bowl as needed.
6. Spoon about 2 teaspoons of filling onto the flat sides of half of the cookies. Assemble the sandwiches with the remaining cookies and enjoy.

FOR THE COOKIES

⅔ cup (150 g) unsalted butter, softened

½ cup (100 g) sugar

2 (30 g) egg yolks

2 teaspoons (10 ml) pure vanilla extract

⅔ cup (150 ml) whole milk

3½ cups (420 g) all-purpose flour, plus more as needed

1 teaspoon (4 g) baking powder

½ teaspoon (3 g) table salt

FOR THE FILLING

2 cups walnuts

½ cup Nutella

2 tablespoons cocoa powder

⅔ cup sugar

1 teaspoon pure vanilla extract

¼ cup whole milk

YIELD: 30 Minutes

ACTIVE TIME: 15 Minutes

TOTAL TIME: 2 Hours

½ cup (55 g) pecans

2½ cups (340 g) confectioners' sugar

Pinch of table salt

1 cup (227 g) unsalted butter, chopped

½ teaspoon (2.5 ml) pure vanilla extract

1¾ cups (210 g) all-purpose flour

RUSSIAN TEA COOKIES

Similar to polvorones, Russian tea cookies are slightly richer due to using pecans instead of almonds as the nutty variable.

---

1. Place the pecans, 1 cup (113 g) of the confectioners' sugar, and salt in food processor and blitz until the nuts are finely ground. Add the butter and pulse to incorporate. Add the vanilla and flour and pulse until the mixture comes together as a smooth dough. Transfer the dough to a mixing bowl, cover with plastic wrap, and chill it in the refrigerator for 1 hour.

2. Preheat the oven to 350°F. Form tablespoons of the dough into balls and place them on unlined, ungreased sheet pans, making sure to leave 1 inch between them. Place one pan of cookies in the oven at a time. Bake until they are a light golden brown, 12 to 14 minutes, rotating the pans halfway through.

3. Remove the cookies from the oven and let them cool on the pans for a few minutes. Place the remaining confectioners' sugar in a shallow bowl and roll the cookies in it until they are completely coated. Transfer the cookies to wire racks and let them cool completely before enjoying.

YIELD: 24 Cookies
ACTIVE TIME: 15 Minutes
TOTAL TIME: 1 Hour

SPICED ESPRESSO COOKIES

Autumn flavors make their way into these pleasantly bittersweet, subtly spiced cookies.

¾ cup (170 g) unsalted butter, softened

⅔ cup (130 g) sugar

2 tablespoons (40 ml) light corn syrup

3 (150 g) eggs

⅓ cup (70 ml) brewed espresso or strong coffee, cooled

1⅔ cups (200 g) all-purpose flour

¾ cup (70 g) almond flour

1 teaspoon (4.5 g) baking soda

⅛ teaspoon (0.5 g) table salt

Pinch of ground cloves

½ teaspoon (1 g) cinnamon

---

1. Preheat the oven to 350°F and line two sheet pans with parchment paper. In the work bowl of a stand mixer fitted with the paddle attachment, cream the butter, sugar, and corn syrup on medium speed until the mixture is very light and fluffy, 2 to 3 minutes, scraping down the work bowl as necessary.
2. Add the eggs one at a time and beat until incorporated, again scraping the work bowl as necessary. Scrape down the work bowl, add the espresso and beat to incorporate. Add the flours, baking soda, salt, cloves, and cinnamon and work the mixture until it comes together as a smooth dough. Let the dough rest for 5 to 10 minutes.
3. Form tablespoons of the dough into balls and arrange them on the pans, making sure to leave 1 inch between them. Place one pan of cookies in the oven at a time. Bake until their edges are set, 12 to 14 minutes, rotating the pans halfway through.
4. Remove the cookies from the oven and let them cool on the pans for a few minutes. Transfer the cookies to a wire rack and let them cool completely before enjoying.

YIELD: 24 Cookies
ACTIVE TIME: 20 Minutes
TOTAL TIME: 1 Hour

PEANUT BUTTER & JAM THUMBPRINTS

For the inner child that still exists in each and every one of us.

½ cup (113 g) unsalted butter, softened

1 cup (270 g) creamy peanut butter

1⅓ cups (280 g) light brown sugar

1 (50 g) egg

½ teaspoon (5 ml) pure vanilla extract

1 cup (120 g) all-purpose flour

1 teaspoon (4.5 g) baking soda

Pinch of table salt

1½ cups (350 g) raspberry jam

---

1. Preheat the oven to 350°F and line two sheet pans with parchment paper. In the work bowl of a stand mixer fitted with the paddle attachment, cream the butter, peanut butter, and brown sugar on medium speed until the mixture is very light and fluffy, 2 to 3 minutes, scraping down the work bowl as necessary.
2. Add the egg and vanilla and beat to incorporate, again scraping the work bowl as necessary. Add the flour, baking soda, and salt and beat until the mixture comes together as a smooth dough. Let the dough rest for 5 to 10 minutes.
3. Form tablespoons of the dough into balls and arrange them on the pans, making sure to leave 1 inch between them. Make an indentation in the centers of the cookies. Place one pan of cookies in the oven at a time. Bake until they are golden brown and their edges are set, 10 to 12 minutes, rotating the pans halfway through.
4. Remove the cookies from the oven and let them cool on the pans for a few minutes. Transfer the cookies to wire racks and let them cool completely.
5. While the cookies are cooling, place the raspberry jam in a saucepan and cook over medium heat, stirring frequently, until the jam has reduced by one-third.
6. Spoon 2 teaspoons of jam into the indentation in each cookie and let it set before enjoying.

PEANUT BUTTER & JAM THUMBPRINTS
page 271

YIELD: 24 Cookies
ACTIVE TIME: 15 Minutes
TOTAL TIME: 1 Hour

PEPAS

Featuring quince jelly and a biscuity base, pepas are a favored treat in Argentina.

½ cup (113 g) unsalted butter, softened

½ cup plus 1 tablespoon (113 g) sugar

1 (50 g) egg

1 (14 g) egg yolk

2 teaspoons (10 ml) pure vanilla extract

Zest of 1 lemon

2¼ cups (270 g) all-purpose flour

Pinch of table salt

¼ cup (85 g) quince jelly

---

1. Preheat the oven to 350°F and line two sheet pans with parchment paper. In the work bowl of a stand mixer fitted with the paddle attachment, cream the butter and sugar on medium speed until the mixture is very light and fluffy, 2 to 3 minutes, scraping down the work bowl as necessary.
2. Add the egg, egg yolk, vanilla, and lemon zest and beat to incorporate, again scraping the work bowl as necessary. Add the flour and salt and beat until the mixture comes together as a smooth dough. Let the dough rest for 5 to 10 minutes.
3. Form tablespoons of the dough into balls and arrange them on the pans, making sure to leave 1 inch between them. Coat the bottom of a measuring cup with nonstick cooking spray and use it to gently press down on each cookie, flattening them slightly. Make an indentation in the centers of the cookies and place some of the quince jelly in each one.
4. Place one pan of cookies in the oven at a time. Bake until they are golden brown and their edges are set, 10 to 12 minutes, rotating the pans halfway through.
5. Remove the cookies from the oven and let them cool on the pans for a few minutes. Transfer the cookies to wire racks and let them cool completely before enjoying.

YIELD: 18 Cookies
ACTIVE TIME: 15 Minutes
TOTAL TIME: 1 Hour

TAHINI, CHOCOLATE & PISTACHIO COOKIES

Incorporating tahini into the dough produces an appealingly moist and chewy result.

1½ cups (145 g) almond flour

½ teaspoon (2 g) baking soda

¼ teaspoon (1 g) table salt

⅔ cup (140 g) light brown sugar

⅓ cup (85 g) tahini paste

1 teaspoon (5 ml) pure vanilla extract

¾ cup (90 g) shelled pistachios, chopped

2 tablespoons (20 g) sesame seeds

1 cup (170 g) chocolate chunks

---

1. Preheat the oven to 350°F and line two sheet pans with parchment paper. In a mixing bowl, combine the almond flour, baking soda, and salt. In the work bowl of a stand mixer fitted with the paddle attachment, beat the brown sugar, tahini, and vanilla until the mixture is smooth and thick. With the mixer running, gradually add the dry mixture and stir until the resulting mixture comes together as a smooth dough. Add the pistachios, sesame seeds, and chocolate chunks and beat until they are evenly distributed. Let the dough rest for 5 to 10 minutes.

2. Form tablespoons of the dough into balls and arrange them on the pans, making sure to leave 1 inch between them. Place one pan of cookies in the oven at a time. Bake until their edges are set and golden brown, 10 to 12 minutes, rotating the pans halfway through.

3. Remove the cookies from the oven and let them cool on the pans for a few minutes. Transfer the cookies to wire racks and let them cool completely before enjoying.

PRESSING MATTERS

While little could be easier than slipping a dough into a piping bag, these cookies do nothing to betray that ease once out of the oven, possessing a composed and elegant look that shall prove irresistible to all who encounter them. They are also among the lightest recipes in the book, and thus ideal for those who are looking for something sweet that can satisfy a craving but not throw a day or a diet out of whack.

YIELD: 24 Macaroons
ACTIVE TIME: 45 Minutes
TOTAL TIME: 3 Hours

COCONUT MACAROONS

For those who love coconut, these sweet, pillowy, and slightly crispy treats are the jewel of their obsession.

1 (14 oz./400 ml) can of sweetened condensed milk

2½ cups (200 g) sweetened shredded coconut

2½ cups (200 g) unsweetened shredded coconut

¼ teaspoon (1 g) table salt

½ teaspoon (2.5 ml) pure vanilla extract

2 (60 g) egg whites

---

1. Line two sheet pans with parchment paper. In a mixing bowl, mix the condensed milk, shredded coconut, salt, and vanilla together with a rubber spatula until combined. Set the mixture aside.
2. In the work bowl of a stand mixer fitted with the whisk attachment, whip the egg whites until they hold stiff peaks. Add the whipped egg whites to the coconut mixture and fold to incorporate.
3. Spoon the dough into a piping bag fitted with a fluted tip and pipe rings of the dough onto the pans, making sure to leave 1 inch between them. Place the pans in the refrigerator and chill the cookies for 1 hour.
4. Preheat the oven to 350°F. Place one pan of cookies in the oven at a time. Bake until they are lightly golden brown, about 20 minutes, rotating the pans halfway through.
5. Remove the cookies from the oven and let them cool completely on the pans before enjoying.

YIELD: 24 Cookies

ACTIVE TIME: 15 Minutes

TOTAL TIME: 2 Hours and 30 Minutes

½ cup (113 g) unsalted butter, softened

⅔ cup (135 g) sugar

¼ cup (80 g) hazelnut paste

½ cup (113 g) cream cheese, softened

2 (30 g) egg yolks

1⅓ cups (160 g) all-purpose flour

½ cup (40 g) unsweetened cocoa powder

2 tablespoons (14 g) cornstarch

½ cup (60 g) shelled pistachios, chopped

Chocolate Ganache (see page 351), warm

NOUGAT WREATHS

With candy bar–levels of chewiness and crunch, these easy-to-prepare cookies are certain to satisfy all who are fortunate enough to encounter them.

---

1. Preheat the oven to 350°F and line two sheet pans with parchment paper. In the work bowl of a stand mixer fitted with the paddle attachment, cream the butter, sugar, hazelnut paste, and cream cheese on medium speed until the mixture is very light and fluffy, 2 to 3 minutes, scraping down the work bowl as necessary.
2. Add the egg yolks and beat to incorporate, again scraping the work bowl as necessary. Add the flour, cocoa powder, and cornstarch and beat until the mixture comes together as a smooth dough. Add the pistachios and beat until they are evenly distributed. Spoon the dough into a piping bag fitted with a fluted tip and pipe rings of the dough onto the pans, making sure to leave 1 inch between them. Place the pans in the refrigerator and chill the cookies for 1 hour.
3. Preheat the oven to 350°F. Place one pan of cookies in the oven at a time. Bake until they are set, 12 to 14 minutes, rotating the pans halfway through.
4. Remove the cookies from the oven and let them cool completely on the pans.
5. When the cookies have cooled, dip them halfway into the ganache and let it set before enjoying.

YIELD: 20 Meringues

ACTIVE TIME: 20 Minutes

TOTAL TIME: 3 Hours and 30 Minutes

½ cup (95 g) caster (superfine) sugar

1 tablespoon (5 g) unsweetened cocoa powder

2 (60 g) egg whites

Pinch of table salt

½ teaspoon (2 g) cream of tartar

CHOCOLATE MERINGUES

These are wonderful on their own, but also incredibly versatile—if you're looking to impress, consider incorporating toasted pine nuts or crushed pink peppercorns into the meringues before baking.

---

1. Preheat the oven to 250°F and line two sheet pans with parchment paper. Place the sugar and cocoa powder in a mixing bowl and whisk to combine. Place the egg whites and salt in the work bowl of a stand mixer fitted with the whisk attachment and whip at high speed until the mixture holds stiff peaks. Add the cream of tartar and whip to incorporate. With the mixer running, incorporate the sugar mixture 1 tablespoon at a time. Whip until the mixture is thick and glossy.
2. Spoon the mixture into a piping bag fitted with fluted tip. Pipe the meringue onto the pans, making sure to leave 1 inch between them.
3. Place the meringues in the oven and bake until they are dry to the touch and sound hollow when lightly tapped, about 1 hour and 45 minutes. Turn off the oven, open the oven door, and let the meringues cool in the oven for 1 hour.
4. After 1 hour, remove them from the oven, transfer them to a wire rack, and let the meringues cool completely before enjoying.

YIELD: 20 Cookies
ACTIVE TIME: 15 Minutes
TOTAL TIME: 1 Hour and 15 Minutes

LEMON & RASPBERRY CLOUDS

This delectable gluten-free cookie will have everyone begging for the recipe.

¾ cup (85 g) raspberries

2 cups plus 2 tablespoons (240 g) confectioners' sugar

4 (120 g) egg whites

2 teaspoons (10 ml) fresh lemon juice

2 cups (190 g) almond flour

3 tablespoons (40 g) pink sanding sugar

---

1. Preheat the oven to 325°F and line two sheet pans with parchment paper. Puree the raspberries in a food processor and strain them through a fine-mesh sieve into a mixing bowl. Add 2 tablespoons (14 g) of confectioners' sugar and stir to combine.

2. In the work bowl of a stand mixer fitted with the whisk attachment, whip the egg whites and lemon juice until combined. With the mixer running on high, gradually add the remaining confectioners' sugar and whip until the mixture comes together as a stiff, glossy meringue. Add the almond flour and raspberry puree and fold until the mixture comes together as a smooth dough.

3. Spoon the mixture into a piping bag fitted with a round tip and pipe ¾-inch rounds onto the pans, making sure to leave 1 inch between them.

4. Place one pan of cookies in the oven at a time. Bake until they are dry to the touch, 20 to 25 minutes, rotating the pans halfway through.

5. Turn off the oven and crack the oven door open. While the cookies are still warm, sprinkle the sanding sugar over the top. Leave them in the oven and let them cool completely before enjoying.

YIELD: 36 Cookies

ACTIVE TIME: 10 minutes

TOTAL TIME: 1 Hour

PIÑA COLADA COOKIES

The tropics aren't often brought to mind by baked goods, making these cookies a particularly unique treat.

2 (60 g) egg whites

Pinch of table salt

1½ cups (170 g) confectioners' sugar

14 tablespoons (225 g) unsweetened almond paste

1 cup (85 g) unsweetened shredded coconut

4 teaspoons (20 ml) rum

1 tablespoon (15 ml) fresh lime juice

---

1. Preheat the oven to 350°F and line two sheet pans with parchment paper. Place the egg whites and salt in the work bowl of a stand mixer fitted with the whisk attachment and whip at high speed until the mixture holds stiff peaks. Add half of the confectioners' sugar and the almond paste and whip to incorporate. Add the remaining confectioners' sugar, the coconut, rum, and lime juice and whip until the mixture comes together as a smooth dough.
2. Spoon the mixture into a piping bag fitted with fluted tip. Pipe 1 oz. (30 g) portions onto the pans, making sure to leave 1 inch between them. Place one pan of cookies in the oven at a time. Bake until they are a light golden brown and their edges are set, 13 to 16 minutes.
3. Remove the cookies from the oven and let them cool completely on the pans before enjoying.

PIÑA COLADA COOKIES

page 287

3¼ cups (310 g) almond flour

2¾ cups (310 g) confectioners' sugar

8 (240 g) egg whites, at room temperature

Pinch of table salt

1½ cups plus 1 tablespoon (310 g) sugar

½ cup (113 ml) water

2 drops of gel food coloring (optional)

YIELD: 30 Macarons

ACTIVE TIME: 1 Hour

TOTAL TIME: 4 Hours

MACARONS

These photogenic treats have become ubiquitous with the rise of social media, but for once, the tremendous hype proves to be justified.

---

1. Line two sheet pans with parchment paper. Place the almond flour and confectioners' sugar in a food processor and blitz for about 1 minute, until the mixture is thoroughly combined and has a fine texture. Place the mixture in a mixing bowl, add three of the egg whites and the salt, and stir with a rubber spatula until the mixture is almost a paste. Set the mixture aside.
2. Place the sugar and water in a small saucepan. Place a candy thermometer in the saucepan and cook the mixture over high heat.
3. While the syrup is coming to a boil, place the remaining egg whites in the work bowl of a stand mixer fitted with the whisk attachment and whip on medium speed until they hold firm peaks.
4. Cook the syrup until it is 245°F. Remove the pan from heat and carefully add the syrup to the whipped egg whites, slowly pouring it down the side of the work bowl. When all of the syrup has been added, whip the mixture until it is glossy, holds stiff peaks, and has cooled slightly. If desired, stir in the food coloring.
5. Add half of the meringue to the almond flour mixture and fold to incorporate. Fold in the remaining meringue. When incorporated, the batter should be smooth, very glossy, and not too runny.
6. Spoon the batter into a piping bag fitted with a plain tip. Pipe evenly sized rounds onto the pans, leaving an inch of space between each one. You want the rounds to be about the size of a silver dollar (approximately 2 inches wide) when you pipe them onto the sheet; they will spread slightly as they sit. Gently tap each pan to smooth the tops of the macarons. Let the macarons sit at room temperature, uncovered, for 1 hour. This allows a skin to form on them.
7. Preheat the oven to 325°F. Place one pan of macarons in the oven at a time. Bake for 10 minutes, rotate the pans, and let them bake for another 5 minutes. Turn off the oven, crack open the oven door, and let the macarons rest in the oven for 5 minutes.
8. Remove the macarons from the oven, transfer them to a wire rack, and let them cool for 2 hours. When the macarons are completely cool, fill with one of the options on page 292 or any filling that you prefer.

The impossibly delicate texture and dynamic coloring of the macaron only partly explains its surge in popularity. Another attribute leading to its rise is its adaptability, as the macaron can accommodate a large number of fillings, and thus appeal to a wide spectrum of palates. While you shouldn't be afraid to be bold with your filling decisions, always remember to err on the dry side, as wetter fillings, such as whipped cream, will dissolve the cookie. To get your mind working, here are five standard fillings.

CHOCOLATE GANACHE: See page 351.

AMERICAN BUTTERCREAM: In the work bowl of a stand mixer fitted with the paddle attachment, combine 1 lb. unsalted butter, 2 lbs. confectioners' sugar, and ⅛ teaspoon table salt and beat until the mixture is smooth and fluffy, about 5 minutes. Reduce the speed to low, add ¼ cup heavy cream and ½ teaspoon pure vanilla extract, and beat until incorporated.

RASPBERRY BUTTERCREAM: Add ¼ cup of seedless raspberry jam to the American Buttercream and beat until incorporated.

LEMON CURD: Fill a small saucepan halfway with water and bring it to a gentle simmer. Place ¾ cup fresh lemon juice in a small saucepan and warm it over low heat. Combine 4 eggs, ¾ cup sugar, ⅛ teaspoon table salt, and ¼ teaspoon pure vanilla extract in a heat-proof mixing bowl. Place the bowl over the simmering water and whisk the mixture continually until it is 135°F on an instant-read thermometer. When the lemon juice comes to a simmer, gradually add it to the egg mixture while whisking constantly. When all of the lemon juice has been incorporated, whisk the curd until it has thickened and is 155°F. Remove the bowl from heat, add the butter, and stir until thoroughly incorporated. Transfer the curd to a mason jar and let it cool completely before using or storing.

CREAM CHEESE FROSTING: See page 352.

YIELD: 36 Cookies
ACTIVE TIME: 30 Minutes
TOTAL TIME: 24 Hours

MATCHA MACARONS

Incorporating the earthy flavor of matcha into a macaron makes for an eye-catching and unique sweet treat.

FOR THE MACARONS

2 (60 g) egg whites

1 teaspoon (5 ml) fresh lemon juice

1⅓ cups (150 g) confectioners' sugar

1¼ cups (120 g) almond flour

2 tablespoons (10 g) matcha powder

FOR THE FILLING

⅔ cup unsalted butter, softened

½ cup confectioners› sugar

½ cup cream cheese, softened

1 drop of green gel food coloring

1. To begin preparations for the macarons, place the egg whites and lemon juice in the work bowl of a stand mixer fitted with the whisk attachment and whip on high speed until the mixture holds soft peaks. Gradually add the confectioners' sugar and beat until the peaks are stiff and shiny. Add the almond flour and matcha powder and gently fold until the mixture comes together as a smooth, very glossy, and not too runny dough. Transfer the batter to a piping bag fitted with a large round tip.

2. Preheat the oven to 250°F and line two sheet pans with parchment paper. Pipe 1-inch rounds onto the pans, making sure to leave about 1 inch between them. Let them sit for about 20 minutes at room temperature.

3. Place one pan of macarons in the oven at a time. Bake until they are dry to the touch, 18 to 20 minutes, rotating the pans halfway through. Remove the macarons from the oven, leave them on the pans, and let them cool overnight.

4. To prepare the filling, place the butter and confectioners' sugar in the work bowl of a stand mixer fitted with the paddle attachment and beat until combined. Add the cream cheese and food coloring and beat to incorporate. Spoon the mixture into a piping bag fitted with a small star tip. Pipe the filling on the flat side of half of the macarons. Assemble the cookies with the remaining macarons and enjoy.

YIELD: 30 Cookies
ACTIVE TIME: 15 Minutes
TOTAL TIME: 1 Hour

LADYFINGERS

Also known as savoiardi, you are no doubt more familiar with these as the base of tiramisu. But they are also lovely on their own, thanks to the subtly sweet taste and cloudlike texture.

3 (150 g) eggs, yolks and whites separated

½ cup plus 1 tablespoon (110 g) sugar

1 teaspoon (5 ml) pure vanilla extract

Pinch of table salt

⅔ cup (80 g) all-purpose flour, plus more as needed

¾ cup (85 g) confectioners' sugar

---

1. Preheat the oven to 300°F and line two sheet pans with parchment paper. Dust the parchment paper with flour and knock off any excess. Place the egg yolks in a mixing bowl and gradually add the sugar, using a handheld mixer running at high speed to combine them. When the mixture is thick and pale yellow, add the vanilla and beat to incorporate.
2. In the work bowl of a stand mixer fitted with the whisk attachment, beat the egg whites and salt until the mixture holds soft peaks. Scoop one-quarter of the egg white mixture into the egg yolk mixture and sift one-quarter of the flour on top. Fold to combine and repeat until all of the egg white mixture and flour have been incorporated and the resulting mixture is light and airy.
3. Spread the batter on the pans in 4-inch-long strips, making sure to leave 1 inch between them. Sprinkle the confectioners' sugar over the top.
4. Place one pan of cookies in the oven at a time. Bake until they lightly golden brown and just crispy, about 20 minutes, rotating the pans halfway through.
5. Remove the cookies from the oven, transfer them to a wire rack, and let them cool completely before enjoying.

YIELD: 24 Cookies
ACTIVE TIME: 45 Minutes
TOTAL TIME: 4 Hours

VANILLA TUILES

These thin, delicate cookies can be molded into tubes, cups, and small bowls while still warm, and filled with whipped cream, berries, puddings, or a custard.

¾ cup plus 2 tablespoons (100 g) all-purpose flour

5 (150 g) egg whites

1 cup plus 2 tablespoons (130 g) confectioners' sugar

½ teaspoon (2.5 ml) pure vanilla extract

⅔ cup (150 g) unsalted butter

---

1. Sift the flour into a small bowl and set it aside. In a separate bowl, whisk the egg whites, confectioners' sugar, and vanilla until combined. Set the mixture aside.
2. In a small saucepan, melt the butter over low heat. Stir it into the egg white mixture, add the flour, and whisk until the mixture comes together as a smooth batter. Cover the bowl with plastic wrap and chill it in the refrigerator for 2 hours.
3. Preheat the oven to 400°F and line two sheet pans with parchment paper. Scoop the batter into a piping bag fitted with a round tip and pipe ⅔ oz. (20 g) portions of the batter onto the pans, making sure to leave 5 inches between them. Use a small, offset spatula to spread the batter into 4-inch circles. Tap the pan lightly on the counter to remove any air bubbles and level the circles. Sprinkle the pistachios over the tuiles.
4. Place one pan of tuiles in the oven at a time. Bake until their edges begin to curl up, 4 to 5 minutes.
5. Remove the tuiles from the oven. Working quickly, carefully remove the tuiles with the offset spatula and set them over a rolling pin to shape. Once they have been shaped, transfer the tuiles to a wire rack. Let them cool completely before enjoying.

YIELD: 24 Cookies
ACTIVE TIME: 30 Minutes
TOTAL TIME: 4 Hours

CHOCOLATE & PISTACHIO TUILES

½ cup plus 1½ tablespoons (70 g) all-purpose flour

2 tablespoons (10 g) cocoa powder

5 (150 g) egg whites

1 cup plus 2 tablespoons (130 g) confectioners' sugar

½ teaspoon (2.5 ml) pure vanilla extract

⅔ cup (150 g) unsalted butter

2 tablespoons (15 g) finely diced pistachios

For an extra-special treat in the summer, place thin, 5-inch circles of batter on a sheet pan, bake them at 475°F for 2 minutes, and roll them around a wooden citrus reamer to form them into ice cream cones.

---

1. Sift the flour and cocoa powder into a small bowl and set the mixture aside. In a separate bowl, whisk the egg whites, confectioners' sugar, and vanilla until combined. Set the mixture aside.
2. In a small saucepan, melt the butter over low heat. Stir it into the egg white mixture, add the flour mixture, and whisk until the mixture comes together as a smooth batter. Cover the bowl with plastic wrap and chill it in the refrigerator for 2 hours.
3. Preheat the oven to 400°F and line two sheet pans with parchment paper. Scoop the batter into a piping bag fitted with a round tip and pipe ⅔ oz. (20 g) portions of the batter onto the pans, making sure to leave 5 inches between them. Use a small, offset spatula to spread the batter into 4-inch circles. Tap the pan lightly on the counter to remove any air bubbles and level the circles. Sprinkle the pistachios over the tuiles.
4. Place one pan of tuiles in the oven at a time. Bake until their edges begin to curl up, 4 to 5 minutes.
5. Remove the tuiles from the oven. Working quickly, carefully remove the tuiles with the offset spatula and set them over a rolling pin to shape. Once they have been shaped, transfer the tuiles to a wire rack. Let them cool completely before enjoying.

YIELD: 48 Cookies
ACTIVE TIME: 15 Minutes
TOTAL TIME: 45 Minutes

ORANGE SPRITZ

The combination of spritz's buttery blast and nutty finish has made them a holiday staple the world over.

1 cup (227 g) unsalted butter, softened

1 cup (200 g) sugar

1 tablespoon (13 g) light brown sugar

Zest of 1 orange

2 (30 g) egg yolks

2¼ cups (270 g) all-purpose flour

¼ teaspoon (1 g) table salt

¼ teaspoon (1 g) baking soda

Confectioners' sugar, to top

---

1. Preheat oven to 350°F and line three sheet pans with parchment paper. In the work bowl of a stand mixer fitted with the paddle attachment, cream the butter, sugar, brown sugar, and orange zest until the mixture is very light and fluffy, 2 to 3 minutes, scraping down the work bowl as necessary. Add the egg yolks and beat to incorporate, again scraping the work bowl.
2. Sift the flour, salt, and baking soda into a separate mixing bowl. Gradually add the dry mixture to the butter mixture, kneading the resulting mixture until it comes together as a smooth dough. Shape the dough into small logs. Working with one at a time, place them in cookie press and press the desired shapes onto the pans, making sure to leave 1 inch between them.
3. Place one pan of cookies in the oven at a time. Bake until their edges start to brown, 10 to 12 minutes, rotating the pans halfway through.
4. Remove the cookies from the oven and transfer them to wire racks to cool completely. Dust them with confectioners' sugar before enjoying.

YIELD: 24 Cookies
ACTIVE TIME: 20 Minutes
TOTAL TIME: 2 Hours

FIORI DI MANDORLE

If you prefer something slightly sweeter at the center of these, swap out the cherry jam for candied cherries.

---

1. Line two sheet pans with parchment paper. In the work bowl of a stand mixer fitted with the paddle attachment, cream the butter and confectioners' sugar on medium speed until the mixture is very light and fluffy, 2 to 3 minutes, scraping down the work bowl as necessary.
2. Reduce the speed to low, add the egg whites, vanilla, and almond extract gradually, and beat until incorporated. Scrape down the work bowl and beat on medium for 1 minute.
3. Add the flour and salt and beat on low until the mixture comes together as a smooth dough. Transfer it to a piping bag fit with a closed fluted tip. Pipe 2-inch-wide cookies onto the pans, making sure to leave ½ inch between each cookie. Place the pans in the refrigerator and chill the cookies for 1 hour.
4. Preheat the oven to 350°F. Use the butt end of a thin-handled wooden spoon to make a hole in the center of each cookie. Place the jam in a piping bag and cut a ½-inch slit in it. Pipe ½ teaspoon of jam onto the center of each cookie. Gently brush all of the cookies with the egg, making sure not to get any on the jam.
5. Place one pan of cookies in the oven at a time. Bake until the edges are a light golden brown, 12 to 14 minutes, rotating the pans halfway through.
6. Remove the cookies from the oven, transfer them to a wire rack, and let them cool completely before enjoying.

½ cup (113 g) unsalted butter, softened

1½ cups (170 g) confectioners' sugar

2 (60 g) egg whites

1 teaspoon (5 ml) pure vanilla extract

1 teaspoon (5 ml) almond extract

2 cups (240 g) all-purpose flour

½ teaspoon (2 g) table salt

1 (50 g) egg, beaten

1 cup (340 g) cherry jam

1 cup (120 g) all-purpose flour

½ cup (45 g) unsweetened cocoa powder

½ teaspoon (2 g) baking soda

Pinch of table salt

½ cup (113 g) unsalted butter, chopped and softened

¾ cup (200 g) creamy peanut butter, at room temperature

1 cup (200 g) sugar

½ cup (105 g) light brown sugar

1 (50 g) egg

1 teaspoon (5 ml) pure vanilla extract

¼ cup (85 g) raspberry jam

CHOCOLATE, PEANUT BUTTER & RASPBERRY CURLS

A cookie that unites two great pairings: chocolate and peanut butter and peanut butter and jelly.

---

1. Preheat the oven to 375°F and line two sheet pans with parchment paper. Sift the flour, cocoa powder, baking soda, and salt into a mixing bowl and set it aside. In the work bowl of a stand mixer fitted with the paddle attachment, cream the butter, peanut butter, sugar, and brown sugar on medium speed until the mixture is very light and fluffy, 2 to 3 minutes, scraping down the work bowl as necessary.
2. Add the egg and vanilla and beat to incorporate, again scraping the work bowl as necessary. With the mixer running, gradually add the dry mixture and beat until the resulting mixture comes together as a smooth dough. Scoop the dough into a piping bag fit with a closed fluted tip and pipe 2-inch-wide cookies onto the pans, making sure to leave ½ inch between each cookie. Place the pans in the refrigerator and chill the cookies for 1 hour.
3. Use the butt end of a thin-handled wooden spoon to make a hole in the center of each cookie. Spoon 1 teaspoon of jam into each hole. Place one pan of cookies in the oven at a time. Bake until their edges are set, 11 to 13 minutes, rotating the pans halfway through.
4. Remove the cookies from the oven and let them cool on the pans for a few minutes. Transfer the cookies to a wire rack and let them cool completely before enjoying.

2 tablespoons (30 ml) orange juice

¼ teaspoon (1 g) ground saffron

½ cup (113 g) unsalted butter, softened

1⅓ cups (270 g) sugar

Pinch of ground cardamom

Pinch of table salt

1 tablespoon (10 g) light brown sugar

Zest of 1 orange

2 (30 g) egg yolks

2⅓ cups (280 g) all-purpose flour

¼ cup (21 g) almond flour

¼ teaspoon (1 g) baking soda

1½ cups (255 g) dark chocolate chips

salt, brown sugar, and orange zest on medium speed until the mixture is very light and fluffy, 2 to 3 minutes, scraping down the work bowl as necessary.

3. Add the egg yolks and beat to incorporate, again scraping the work bowl as necessary. Sift the flour, almond flour, and baking soda into a separate mixing bowl and whisk to combine. Gradually add the flour mixture to work bowl and beat until the resulting mixture comes together as a dough. Gradually add the saffron-infused orange juice and beat until the dough is smooth. Let the dough rest for 5 to 10 minutes.

4. Place the dough in a piping bag fitted with a fluted tip. Pipe 2½-inch-long strips onto the pans, making sure to leave 1 inch between them. Place one pan of cookies in the oven at a time. Bake until they are golden brown, 10 to 12 minutes, rotating the pans halfway through.

5. Remove the cookies from the oven, transfer them to a wire rack, and let them cool completely.

6. Fill a saucepan halfway with water and bring to a gentle simmer. Place the chocolate chips in a heatproof bowl, place it over the simmering water, and stir until they have melted. Dip one end of the cookies into the melted chocolate and let the chocolate set before enjoying.

YIELD: 30 to 50 Cookies
ACTIVE TIME: 40 Minutes
TOTAL TIME: 40 Minutes

PIZZELLES

Anise extract is traditional here, but consider experimenting with other flavors, as many interesting ones are now available.

1¾ cups (210 g) all-purpose flour, plus more as needed

2 teaspoons (8 g) baking powder

½ teaspoon (2 g) table salt

3 (150 g) eggs

⅔ cup (130 g) sugar

½ cup (113 g) unsalted butter, melted

1 teaspoon (5 ml) pure vanilla extract

½ teaspoon (2.5 ml) anise extract

---

1. Preheat a pizzelle maker. Combine the flour, baking powder, and salt in a small bowl. In the work bowl of a stand mixer fitted with the paddle attachment, beat the eggs and sugar until the mixture is very light and fluffy, 2 to 3 minutes, scraping down the work bowl as necessary. Slowly add the melted butter, vanilla, and anise extract and beat until incorporated, again scraping the work bowl as necessary. Gradually add the dry mixture and beat until the resulting mixture comes together as a smooth batter.
2. Using two spoons, carefully drop the batter onto the center of pizzelle maker (teaspoons for 3-inch pizzelles, and tablespoons for 5-inch cookies).
3. Cook until the pizzelles are just lightly brown, about 30 seconds. Gently remove the cookies from the pizzelle maker, transfer them to a wire rack, and let them cool completely before enjoying.

RAISE THE BAR

You may be thinking: *Wait, these aren't cookies.* While that is technically true, we think of brownies and bars as unfussy, no-less-delicious members of the cookie family, consisting of doughs and batters that require no shaping, a quality that makes them great options for those moments where one needs to soothe a craving in a hurry.

YIELD: 20 to 24 Brownies
ACTIVE TIME: 30 Minutes
TOTAL TIME: 2 Hours

½ lb. (225 g) bittersweet chocolate

1½ cups (340 g) unsalted butter

1¾ cups (350 g) sugar

1¾ cups (360 g) light brown sugar

¼ cup plus 1 tablespoon (25 g) cocoa powder

1 teaspoon (6 g) table salt

5 (250 g) eggs

1½ teaspoons (7.5 ml) pure vanilla extract

2 cups (240 g) all-purpose flour

BROWNIES

Toss aside those store-bought mixes for good, as this recipe for homemade brownies has it all.

---

1. Preheat the oven to 350°F. Line a 9 x 13–inch baking pan with parchment paper and coat it with nonstick cooking spray.
2. Fill a small saucepan halfway with water and bring it to a simmer. Place the chocolate and butter in a heatproof bowl, place it over the simmering water, and stir until they have melted and the mixture is smooth. Remove the bowl from heat and set the mixture aside.
3. In a separate mixing bowl, whisk the sugar, brown sugar, cocoa powder, and salt together, making sure to break up any clumps. Whisk in the eggs, vanilla, and melted chocolate mixture and then gradually add the flour, whisking to thoroughly incorporate each addition.
4. Pour the batter into the baking pan and use a rubber spatula to smooth the top. Lightly tap the pan on the counter to remove any air bubbles.
5. Place the brownies in the oven and bake until a cake tester or a knife inserted into the center comes out clean, 35 to 40 minutes.
6. Remove the brownies from the oven, transfer the pan to a wire rack, and let them cool completely.
7. Cut the brownies into squares or strips and enjoy.

YIELD: 20 to 24 Brownies
ACTIVE TIME: 30 Minutes
TOTAL TIME: 3 Hours

CHOCOLATE CHUNK BROWNIES

Because for some, a double dose of chocolate isn't quite enough.

½ lb. (225 g) dark chocolate (55 to 65 percent)

1½ cups (340 g) unsalted butter

1¾ cups (350 g) sugar

1¾ cups (360 g) light brown sugar

¼ cup plus 1 tablespoon (25 g) unsweetened cocoa powder

1 teaspoon (6 g) table salt

5 (250 g) eggs

1½ teaspoons (7.5 ml) pure vanilla extract

2 cups (240 g) all-purpose flour

1 cup (170 g) chopped milk chocolate

---

1. Preheat the oven to 350°F. Line a 9 x 13–inch baking pan with parchment paper and coat it with nonstick cooking spray.
2. Fill a small saucepan halfway with water and bring it to a simmer. Place the dark chocolate and butter in a heatproof bowl, place it over the simmering water, and stir until they have melted and the mixture is smooth. Remove the bowl from heat and set the mixture aside.
3. In a separate mixing bowl, whisk the sugar, brown sugar, cocoa powder, and salt together, making sure to break up any clumps. Whisk in the eggs, vanilla, and melted chocolate mixture and then gradually add the flour, whisking to thoroughly incorporate each addition. Add the milk chocolate and stir until it is evenly distributed.
4. Pour the batter into the baking pan and use a rubber spatula to smooth the top. Lightly tap the pan on the counter to remove any air bubbles.
5. Place the brownies in the oven and bake until a cake tester or a knife inserted into the center comes out clean, 35 to 40 minutes.
6. Remove the brownies from the oven, transfer the pan to a wire rack, and let them cool completely.
7. Cut the brownies into squares or strips and enjoy.

YIELD: 16 Brownies

ACTIVE TIME: 15 Minutes

TOTAL TIME: 1 Hour and 15 Minutes

STOUT BROWNIES

The wonderfully bitter richness of a stout is capable of transforming an otherwise straightforward brownie batter.

1½ cups (340 ml) Guinness or other stout

1 cup (227 g) unsalted butter, softened

2 cups (340 g) bittersweet chocolate chips

1½ cups (300 g) sugar

3 (150 g) eggs

1 teaspoon (5 ml) pure vanilla extract

2 cups (240 g) all-purpose flour

1¼ teaspoons (6 g) table salt

---

1. Preheat the oven to 350°F and coat a square 9-inch baking pan with nonstick cooking spray. Place the stout in a medium saucepan and bring to a boil. Cook until it has reduced by half. Remove pan from the heat and let the stout cool.
2. Fill a small saucepan halfway with water and bring it to a gentle simmer. Place the butter and chocolate chips in a heatproof bowl, place it over the simmering water, and stir until they have melted and the mixture is smooth. Remove the bowl from heat and let the mixture cool for 5 minutes.
3. Place the sugar, eggs, and vanilla in a large bowl and stir until combined. While stirring, slowly add the melted chocolate-and-butter mixture and then the stout.
4. Add the flour and salt and fold until the mixture comes together as a smooth batter. Pour the batter into the pan and gently tap it on the counter to remove any air bubbles.
5. Place the brownies in the oven and bake until the surface begins to crack and a cake tester inserted into the center comes out with a few moist crumbs attached, 35 to 40 minutes.
6. Remove the pan from the oven, place it on a wire rack, and let the brownies cool completely. Cut them into squares or strips and enjoy.

YIELD: 12 Brownies

ACTIVE TIME: 30 Minutes

TOTAL TIME: 2 Hours and 45 Minutes

FLOURLESS FUDGE BROWNIES

No flour? No problem—these cakey brownies will keep you from panicking when you discover your pantry isn't as well stocked as you thought.

1 lb. (450 g) semisweet chocolate, chopped

1 cup (227 g) unsalted butter

1¾ cups (350 g) sugar

⅔ cup (140 g) light brown sugar

¼ cup (20 g) unsweetened cocoa powder

¾ teaspoon (4 g) table salt

6 (300 g) eggs

1½ teaspoons (7.5 ml) pure vanilla extract

---

1. Preheat the oven to 350°F. Line a 9 x 13–inch baking pan with parchment paper and coat it with nonstick cooking spray.
2. Fill a small saucepan halfway with water and bring it to a simmer. Place the chocolate and butter in a heatproof bowl, place it over the simmering water, and stir until they have melted and the mixture is smooth. Remove the bowl from heat and set the mixture aside.
3. In a separate mixing bowl, whisk the sugar, brown sugar, cocoa powder, and salt together, making sure to break up any clumps. Whisk in the eggs, vanilla, and melted chocolate mixture until the resulting mixture comes together as a smooth batter.
4. Pour the batter into the pan and use a rubber spatula to smooth the top. Lightly tap the baking pan on the counter to remove any air bubbles.
5. Place the brownies in the oven and bake until a cake tester inserted into the center comes out clean, 30 to 40 minutes.
6. Remove the brownies from the oven, transfer the pan to a wire rack, and let the brownies cool completely.
7. Cut the brownies into squares or strips and enjoy.

YIELD: 12 Brownies
ACTIVE TIME: 15 Minutes
TOTAL TIME: 1 Hour and 15 Minutes

MARBLE BROWNIES

You can also produce the swirled mix of batters in the mixing bowl, but we've found that doing it in the pan produces the ideal amount of contrast between them.

---

1. Preheat the oven to 350°F. Coat a square 9-inch baking pan with nonstick cooking spray and dust it with flour, knocking out any excess.
2. Fill a small saucepan halfway with water and bring it to a gentle simmer. Place the butter and chocolate chips in a heatproof bowl, place it over the simmering water, and stir until they have melted and the mixture is smooth. Remove the bowl from heat and let the mixture cool.
3. Place 2 of the eggs and three-quarters of the sugar in in the work bowl of a stand mixer fitted with the paddle attachment and beat on medium speed for 1 minute. Add the melted chocolate mixture, beat for 1 minute, and then add the flour and salt. Beat until the resulting mixture just comes together as a smooth batter. Pour it into the pan.
4. In the work bowl of a stand mixer fitted with the paddle attachment, cream the cream cheese, remaining sugar, remaining egg, and vanilla on medium speed until the mixture is light and fluffy, 2 to 3 minutes, scraping down the work bowl as necessary.
5. Spread the cream cheese mixture on top of the batter in the pan and use a rubber spatula or fork to swirl the mixtures.
6. Place the brownies in the oven and bake until the top is springy to the touch and a cake tester inserted into the center comes out clean, 35 to 40 minutes.
7. Remove the brownies from the oven, transfer the pan to a wire rack, and let them cool completely.
8. Cut the brownies into squares or strips and enjoy.

1 cup (120 g) all-purpose flour, plus more as needed dusting

1 cup (227 g) unsalted butter

½ cup (85 g) semisweet chocolate chips

6 (300 g) eggs

2 cups (400 g) sugar

Pinch of table salt

1 cup (227 g) cream cheese, softened

½ teaspoon (2.5 ml) pure vanilla extract

½ lb. (225 g) white chocolate

1½ cups (340 g) unsalted butter

1¾ cups (350 g) sugar

¾ cup (360 g) light brown sugar

1 teaspoon (6 g) table salt

5 (250 g) eggs

1½ teaspoons (7.5 ml) pure vanilla extract

2 cups (240 g) all-purpose flour

¾ cup (90 g) raspberries

YIELD: 12 to 24 Bars

ACTIVE TIME: 15 Minutes

TOTAL TIME: 1 Hour

WHITE CHOCOLATE & RASPBERRY BROWNIES

Yes, they look like blondies, but once you encounter their rich, moist character, you'll know that brownie is the correct characterization for these treats.

---

1. Preheat the oven to 350°F. Line a 9 x 13–inch baking pan with parchment paper and coat it with nonstick cooking spray.
2. Fill a small saucepan halfway with water and bring it to a simmer. Place the white chocolate and butter in a heatproof bowl, place it over the simmering water, and stir until they have melted and the mixture is smooth. Remove the bowl from heat and set the mixture aside.
3. In a separate mixing bowl, whisk the sugar, brown sugar, and salt together, making sure to break up any clumps. Whisk in the eggs, vanilla, and melted chocolate mixture and then gradually add the flour, whisking to thoroughly incorporate before adding the next bit. Add the raspberries and stir until they are evenly distributed.
4. Pour the batter into the baking pan and use a rubber spatula to smooth the top. Lightly tap the baking pan on the counter to remove any air bubbles.
5. Place the brownies in the oven and bake until a cake tester or a knife inserted into the center comes out clean, 35 to 40 minutes.
6. Remove the brownies from the oven, transfer the pan to a wire rack, and let them cool completely.
7. Cut the brownies into squares and enjoy.

YIELD: 12 to 16 Blondies
ACTIVE TIME: 30 Minutes
TOTAL TIME: 2 Hours

BLONDIES

The ideal base for whatever blondie visions you have.

¾ cup (170 g) unsalted butter

1 cup (210 g) light brown sugar

¾ teaspoon (2 g) table salt

2 (100 g) eggs

1½ teaspoon (7.5 ml) pure vanilla extract

1 cup (120 g) all-purpose flour

½ teaspoon (2 g) baking powder

½ teaspoon (2 g) baking soda

---

1. Preheat the oven to 350°F. Line a square 9-inch baking pan with parchment paper and coat it with nonstick cooking spray.
2. Place the butter in a small saucepan and melt it over medium heat. Remove the pan from heat and let the butter cool slightly.
3. In a mixing bowl, whisk the brown sugar and salt together, making sure to break up any clumps. Whisk in the eggs, vanilla, and melted butter and then gradually add the flour, whisking to thoroughly incorporate each addition. Add the baking powder and baking soda and whisk to combine.
4. Pour the batter into the baking pan and use a rubber spatula to smooth the top. Lightly tap the pan on the counter to remove any air bubbles.
5. Place the blondies in the oven and bake until a cake tester or a knife inserted into the center comes out clean, 35 to 40 minutes.
6. Remove the blondies from the oven, transfer the pan to a wire rack, and let them cool completely.
7. Cut the blondies into squares or strips and enjoy.

YIELD: 12 to 16 Bars

ACTIVE TIME: 30 Minutes

TOTAL TIME: 2 Hours

LEMON BLONDIES

Light, chewy, and delightfully lemony, these blondies are wonderful at a summer barbecue.

¾ cup (170 g) unsalted butter

1 cup (200 g) sugar

¾ teaspoon (2 g) table salt

2 (100 g) eggs

Zest of 1 lemon

1 tablespoon (15 ml) fresh lemon juice

1 cup (120 g) all-purpose flour

½ teaspoon (2 g) baking powder

½ teaspoon (2 g) baking soda

Confectioners' sugar, to top

---

1. Preheat the oven to 350°F. Line a square 9-inch baking pan with parchment paper and coat it with nonstick cooking spray.
2. Place the butter in a small saucepan and melt it over medium heat. Remove the pan from heat and let the butter cool slightly.
3. In a mixing bowl, whisk the sugar and salt together. Whisk in the eggs, lemon zest, lemon juice, and melted butter and then gradually add the flour, whisking to thoroughly incorporate each addition. Add the baking powder and baking soda and whisk to combine.
4. Pour the batter into the baking pan and use a rubber spatula to smooth the top. Lightly tap the pan on the counter to remove any air bubbles.
5. Place the blondies in the oven and bake until a cake tester or a knife inserted into the center comes out clean, 35 to 40 minutes.
6. Remove the blondies from the oven, transfer the pan to a wire rack, and let them cool completely.
7. Dust the blondies with confectioners' sugar. Cut the blondies into squares or strips and enjoy.

YIELD: 16 to 20 Bars

ACTIVE TIME: 20 Minutes

TOTAL TIME: 2 Hours

RASPBERRY BARS

When berry season is at its peak, turn to these delectable bars.

2 balls of piecrust dough

¾ cup (90 g) all-purpose flour, plus more as needed

7 cups (840) fresh raspberries

2 cups (400 g) sugar

2 tablespoons (30 ml) fresh lemon juice

Pinch of table salt

1 egg, beaten

Confectioners' sugar, to top

1. Preheat the oven to 350°F and coat a rimmed sheet pan with nonstick cooking spray. Roll out one of the balls of dough on flour-dusted work surface so that it fits the pan. Place it in the pan, press down to ensure that it is even, and prick it all over with a fork. Roll out the other crust so that it is slightly larger than the sheet.
2. Place the raspberries, sugar, flour, lemon juice, and salt in a mixing bowl and stir until well combined, mashing the raspberries as you stir. Spread this mixture evenly over the crust in the pan.
3. Place the top crust over the filling and trim away any excess. Brush the top crust with the egg and place the bars in the oven. Bake until they are golden brown, about 40 minutes.
4. Remove the bars from the oven and let them cool completely before slicing them into squares or strips and enjoying.

1¼ cups (150 g) all-purpose flour

⅓ cup (65 g) sugar

1 cup (227 g) unsalted butter, cubed, plus more as needed

1 (14 oz./400 ml) can of condensed milk

½ cup (105 g) light brown sugar

2 tablespoons (40 ml) light corn syrup

1¼ cups (210 g) chopped semisweet chocolate

YIELD: 12 to 16 Bars

ACTIVE TIME: 15 Minutes

TOTAL TIME: 2 Hours and 30 Minutes

CHOCOLATE-COVERED TOFFEE BARS

A Heath bar, made entirely at home.

---

1. Coat a square 9-inch baking pan with butter. Combine the flour, sugar, and ½ cup (113 g) of the butter in a food processor and pulse until the mixture resembles coarse bread crumbs. Press the mixture into the pan, making sure that it is even, prick it all over with a fork, and chill the crust in the refrigerator for 30 minutes.
2. Preheat the oven to 350°F. Place the crust in the oven and bake until it just starts to turn golden brown, about 20 minutes. Remove the crust from the oven and let it cool in the pan.
3. Place the condensed milk, brown sugar, corn syrup, and remaining butter in a large saucepan and bring to a boil, stirring continually. Cook, stirring frequently, until the mixture has thickened, about 5 minutes. Remove the pan from the heat and let the toffee cool for 5 minutes.
4. Pour the toffee over the crust in the pan and let it cool for 30 minutes.
5. Fill a small saucepan halfway with water and bring it to a simmer. Place the chocolate in a heatproof bowl, place it over the simmering water, and stir until the chocolate has melted.
6. Remove the pan from heat and pour the melted chocolate over the toffee, using a rubber spatula to spread it out evenly. Cover the pan with plastic wrap and chill the bars in the refrigerator until the chocolate has set, about 30 minutes.
7. Cut the bars into squares or strips and enjoy.

YIELD: 12 to 16 Bars

ACTIVE TIME: 15 Minutes

TOTAL TIME: 2 Hours

FIG BARS

Experiment with hazelnut and chickpea flour in place of the almond flour here, as each will shift the flavor and texture of these bars in a direction that might just be a perfect match for your palate.

1 cup (227 g) unsalted butter, chilled and cubed

½ cup (100 g) sugar

¼ teaspoon (1 g) table salt

1¾ cups (210 g) all-purpose flour, plus more as needed

¾ cup (70 g) almond flour

1 cup (113 g) rolled oats

3 tablespoons (45 ml) whole milk

2 cups (170 g) fig jam

---

1. In the work bowl of a stand mixer fitted with the paddle attachment, cream the butter and sugar on medium speed until the mixture is very light and fluffy, 2 to 3 minutes, scraping down the work bowl as necessary. Add the salt, flours, oats, and milk and beat until the mixture comes together as a smooth dough. Form the dough into a disk, cover it with plastic wrap, and chill it in the refrigerator for 30 minutes.

2. Preheat the oven to 350°F. Line a square 9-inch baking pan with parchment paper, making sure two sides are overhanging. Divide the dough in half, place the pieces on a flour-dusted work surface, and roll them out into 9-inch squares that are about ¼ inch thick. Press one square of dough into the base of the pan and prick it all over with a fork. Spread the fig jam evenly over the dough, lay the remaining piece of dough on top, and gently press down on it.

3. Prick the top piece of dough all over with a fork, place the pan in the oven, and bake until the top of the bars is golden brown and dry to the touch, 35 to 45 minutes.

4. Remove the bars from the oven, place the pan on a wire rack, and let them cool completely. Cut the bars into squares or strips and enjoy.

YIELD: 12 Bars

ACTIVE TIME: 1 Hour

TOTAL TIME: 3 Hours and 30 Minutes

PEPPERMINT BARS

This recipe will certainly be popular around the holidays, but its refreshing, comforting qualities will work any time of year.

---

1. Preheat the oven to 350°F. Line a 9 x 13–inch baking pan with parchment paper and coat it with nonstick cooking spray. To begin preparations for the crust, fill a small saucepan halfway with water and bring it to a simmer. Place the chocolate and butter in a heatproof bowl, place it over the simmering water, and stir until they have melted and the mixture is smooth. Remove the bowl from heat and set the mixture aside.

2. In a mixing bowl, whisk the sugar, brown sugar, cocoa powder, and salt together, making sure to break up any clumps. Add the eggs and vanilla, whisk to incorporate, and then add the melted chocolate mixture. Whisk to incorporate, pour the batter into the baking pan, and smooth the surface with a rubber spatula. Lightly tap the baking pan on the counter to settle the batter and remove any air bubbles.

3. Place the crust in the oven and bake until a cake tester inserted into the center comes out clean, 20 to 30 minutes. Remove the crust from the oven and transfer the pan to a wire rack. Let the crust cool completely.

4. To prepare the topping, place the confectioners' sugar, butter, and cream in the work bowl of a stand mixer fitted with the paddle attachment and beat on low until the mixture just comes together. Raise the speed to medium and beat until the mixture is light and fluffy, 2 to 3 minutes, scraping down the work bowl as necessary. Add the peppermint candies and beat until they are evenly distributed.

5. Spread the mixture over the baked crust, using a rubber spatula to smooth the top. Transfer the pan to the refrigerator and chill until the topping is set, about 2 hours.

6. Run a sharp knife along the edge of the pan and carefully remove the bars. Place them on a cutting board and cut them into squares or strips. Drizzle the ganache over the bars, sprinkle the additional peppermint candies on top, and store the bars in the refrigerator until ready to serve.

FOR THE CRUST

½ lb. (250 g) semisweet chocolate, chopped

½ cup (113 g) unsalted butter

¾ cup plus 1½ tablespoons (170 g) sugar

¼ cup plus 1 tablespoon (60 g) light brown sugar

2 tablespoons (10 g) unsweetened cocoa powder

¼ teaspoon (1 g) table salt

3 (150 g) eggs

¾ teaspoon (4 ml) pure vanilla extract

FOR THE TOPPING

7 cups confectioners' sugar

6 tablespoons unsalted butter, softened

½ cup heavy cream

2 cups peppermint candy pieces, plus more to top

Chocolate Ganache (see page 351), warm

YIELD: 20 to 24 Bars
ACTIVE TIME: 45 Minutes
TOTAL TIME: 24 Hours

PUMPKIN CHEESECAKE BARS

Thanks to these reasonably sized bars, now you don't have to worry about indulging in cheesecake.

FOR THE CRUST

2 cups (200 g) graham cracker crumbs

¼ cup (50 g) sugar

½ cup (113 g) unsalted butter

FOR THE TOPPING

1½ lbs. cream cheese, softened

1 cup sugar

¾ cup light brown sugar

6 eggs

1 tablespoon pure vanilla extract

1½ teaspoons pumpkin pie spice

1 (14 oz.) can of pumpkin puree

Whipped Cream (see page 357), to top

Cinnamon, to top

1. Preheat the oven to 325°F. Line a 9 x 13–inch baking pan with parchment paper, making sure two sides overhang, and coat it with nonstick cooking spray. To prepare the crust, place all of the ingredients in a mixing bowl and work the mixture with your hands until it is combined, soft, and crumbly.
2. Firmly press the crust into the pan, making sure it is flat and even. Place it in the oven and bake until the crust begins to brown at the edges, about 20 minutes. Remove the crust from the oven and place the pan on a wire rack. Let the crust cool completely.
3. To prepare the topping, place the cream cheese, sugar, and brown sugar in a mixing bowl and stir to combine. Add the eggs and vanilla and stir to incorporate. Add the pumpkin pie spice and pumpkin puree and stir until thoroughly combined.
4. Spread the topping over the crust, smooth the top with a rubber spatula, and place the pan in the oven. Bake until the edges of the filling appear set and the center jiggles slightly when you shake the pan.
5. Remove the cheesecake bars from the oven and let them cool completely. Chill the bars in the refrigerator overnight.
6. Remove the bars from the refrigerator, use the parchment paper to lift them out of the pan, and cut them into squares or strips. Top each bar with some Whipped Cream and cinnamon and serve.

YIELD: 12 to 16 Bars

ACTIVE TIME: 30 Minutes

TOTAL TIME: 2 Hours and 30 Minutes

CRISPY RICE & OAT BARS

Consider dipping these bars into the Coating Chocolate (see page 352), instead of just drizzling the Chocolate Ganache over the top.

3 cups (340 g) rolled oats

6 cups (150 g) crispy rice cereal

1 cup (210 g) light brown sugar

¾ cup (170 g) unsalted butter

¾ cup (250 ml) honey

¼ cup (80 ml) light corn syrup

4 teaspoons (22 g) table salt

2 tablespoons (30 ml) pure vanilla extract

Chocolate Ganache (see page 351), warm

---

1. Place the oats in a medium saucepan, cover them with water, and bring to a simmer. Cook until the oats are just tender, 6 to 8 minutes, stirring occasionally. Drain the oats and let them cool.
2. Line a 9 x 13–inch baking pan with parchment paper and coat it with nonstick cooking spray. Place the cereal and oats in a mixing bowl and stir to combine. Set the mixture aside.
3. In a medium saucepan, combine the brown sugar, butter, honey, corn syrup, and salt. Bring to a boil over medium heat and cook for another 2 minutes. Remove the pan from heat, stir in the vanilla, and then pour the syrup over the cereal mixture. Stir the resulting mixture with a rubber spatula until well combined.
4. Press the mixture into the pan until it is flat and even. Place the pan in the refrigerator and chill the bars for 2 hours.
5. Remove the bars from the refrigerator and cut them into squares or strips. Drizzle the ganache over the bars and let it set before enjoying.

2 cups (170 g) chickpea flour

1 cup (130 g) walnuts, minced, plus whole walnuts to top

¾ cup (170 g) unsalted butter

⅔ cup (205 ml) real maple syrup

1 cup (210 g) light brown sugar

1 teaspoon (5 ml) pure vanilla extract

YIELD: 12 Bars

ACTIVE TIME: 15 Minutes

TOTAL TIME: 1 Hour and 20 Minutes

GLUTEN-FREE MAPLE WALNUT BARS

An old-school combo of flavors gets revitalized in a new-age, gluten-free package.

---

1. Preheat the oven to 350°F. Line a square 9-inch baking pan with parchment paper and coat it with nonstick cooking spray. In a large mixing bowl, combine the flour and walnuts. Place the butter, maple syrup, brown sugar, and vanilla in a saucepan and cook over medium heat, stirring until the butter has melted and the brown sugar has dissolved.
2. Pour the butter mixture over the flour mixture and stir until the mixture is thoroughly combined. Transfer the mixture to the pan and press down until it is packed into a firm, even layer.
3. Place the bars in the oven and bake until they are browned on top and a cake tester inserted into the center comes out with a few moist crumbs attached, 30 to 40 minutes.
4. Remove the bars from the oven and let the bars cool in the pan for 10 minutes.
5. Slice the bars into squares or strips and let them cool completely in the pan before enjoying.

YIELD: 20 to 24 Bars

ACTIVE TIME: 40 Minutes

TOTAL TIME: 5 Hours

LEMON BARS

A confection for those who prefer a fruit-based dessert, and those who aren't afraid of a little tartness at the end of the day.

FOR THE CRUST

2 cups (240 g) all-purpose flour

½ cup plus 2 tablespoons (125 g) sugar

¼ teaspoon (1 g) table salt

1 cup (227 g) unsalted butter, softened

FOR THE TOPPING

2¼ cups sugar

¾ cup all-purpose flour

Zest of 2 lemons

¼ teaspoon table salt

5 eggs

1 cup fresh lemon juice

Confectioners' sugar, to top

---

1. Preheat the oven to 325°F. Line a 9 x 13–inch baking pan with parchment paper and coat it with nonstick cooking spray. To prepare the crust, place all of the ingredients in a mixing bowl and work the mixture with your hands until it is combined, soft, and crumbly. Firmly press the crust into the baking pan, making sure it is flat and even.
2. Place the crust in the oven and bake until it begins to brown at the edges, about 20 minutes. Remove the crust from the oven, place the pan on a wire rack, and let the crust cool completely.
3. To prepare the topping, place the sugar, flour, lemon zest, and salt in a mixing bowl and whisk until combined. Add the eggs and lemon juice, whisk until well combined, and spread the mixture over the baked crust, smoothing the top with a rubber spatula.
4. Place the bars in the oven and bake until the center of the top is set, 20 to 25 minutes.
5. Remove the bars from the oven, transfer the pan to a wire rack, and let them cool for 2 hours.
6. Transfer the bars to the refrigerator and chill them for 2 hours.
7. Cut the bars into squares or strips, dust them with confectioners' sugar, and store them in the refrigerator until ready to serve.

the peanut butter to the milk mixture and stir until well combined. Fold in the oats and stir until they are completely coated. Let the mixture sit for 15 minutes.

4. Line a square 9-inch baking pan with parchment paper and coat it with nonstick cooking spray. Pour the oat mixture into it and press it into an even layer. Spread the remaining melted chocolate over the top and let the chocolate set for 30 minutes.
5. Cut the bars into squares or strips and enjoy.

YIELD: 12 to 16 Bars
ACTIVE TIME: 15 Minutes
TOTAL TIME: 1 Hour

PRALINE BARS

The famed New Orleans treat—which may well have been the first street food sold in America—gets repackaged into a bar.

FOR THE CRUST

1 cup plus 2 tablespoons (255 g) unsalted butter

4 cups (300 g) graham cracker crumbs

3 tablespoons (35 g) sugar

¼ cup plus 1 tablespoon (35 g) all-purpose flour

FOR THE TOPPING

4½ cups light brown sugar

6 eggs

1 cup graham cracker crumbs

1½ teaspoons table salt

¾ teaspoon baking powder

1 tablespoon pure vanilla extract

1½ cups pecans, chopped

---

1. Preheat the oven to 350°F. Line a 9 x 13–inch baking pan with parchment paper and coat it with nonstick cooking spray. To begin preparations for the crust, melt the butter in a small saucepan over medium-low heat. Remove the pan from heat and set the butter aside.
2. In a mixing bowl, combine the graham cracker crumbs, sugar, and flour. Add the melted butter and stir to incorporate. Press the mixture into the pan so that it is flat and even.
3. Place the crust in the oven and bake until it begins to brown at the edges, about 20 minutes. Remove the crust from the oven, place the pan on a wire rack, and let the crust cool completely.
4. To prepare the topping, whisk the brown sugar and eggs together in a mixing bowl until there are no clumps left, about 2 minutes. Add the graham cracker crumbs, salt, baking powder, and vanilla and whisk until thoroughly incorporated. Pour the topping over the crust and evenly distribute the pecans over the top, gently pressing down so they adhere.
5. Place the bars in the oven and bake until the top is golden brown, 25 to 30 minutes.
6. Remove the bars from the oven, transfer the pan to a wire rack, and let them cool.
7. Cut the bars into squares or strips and enjoy.

YIELD: 12 to 16 Bars
ACTIVE TIME: 15 Minutes
TOTAL TIME: 1 Hour

STRAWBERRY STREUSEL BARS

If you're not the biggest fan of streusel-topped treats, simply double the ingredients for the crust, divide the dough into two pieces, and sandwich the strawberry mixture between them.

FOR THE CRUST

1 cup (120 g) all-purpose flour

5 tablespoons (65 g) sugar

Pinch of table salt

½ cup (113 g) unsalted butter, softened

FOR THE TOPPING

6 cups sliced fresh strawberries

2 cups sugar, plus more to top

2 tablespoons fresh lemon juice

Pinch of table salt

Streusel Topping (see page 357)

---

1. Preheat the oven to 350°F. Coat a square 9-inch baking pan with parchment paper and coat it with nonstick cooking spray. To prepare the crust, place all of the ingredients in a mixing bowl and work the mixture with your hands until it is combined, soft, and crumbly. Firmly press the crust into the pan, making sure it is flat and even.
2. Place the crust in the oven and bake until it begins to brown at the edges, about 20 minutes. Remove the crust from the oven, place the pan on a wire rack, and let the crust cool completely.
3. To begin preparations for the topping, place the strawberries, sugar, lemon juice, and salt in a mixing bowl and stir until well combined, mashing the strawberries as you stir. Cover the bowl with a kitchen towel and let the mixture sit for 45 minutes.
4. Spread the strawberry mixture evenly across the crust in the pan. Sprinkle the Streusel Topping over the top.
5. Place the bars in the oven and bake until the top is golden brown, 25 to 30 minutes.
6. Remove the bars from the oven and let them cool.
7. Cut the bars into squares or strips and enjoy.

APPENDIX

VANILLA GLAZE

YIELD: 1½ Cups
ACTIVE TIME: 5 Minutes
TOTAL TIME: 5 Minutes

½ cup whole milk, plus more as needed

¼ teaspoon pure vanilla extract

1 lb. confectioners' sugar, plus more as needed

1. In a mixing bowl, whisk all of the ingredients until combined.
2. If the glaze is too thick, incorporate tablespoons of milk until it reaches the desired consistency. If too thin, incorporate tablespoons of confectioners' sugar. Use immediately, or store in the refrigerator for up to 5 days.

CHOCOLATE GANACHE

YIELD: 1½ Cups
ACTIVE TIME: 10 Minutes
TOTAL TIME: 15 Minutes

½ lb. chocolate

1 cup heavy cream

1. Place the chocolate in a heatproof mixing bowl and set it aside.
2. Place the heavy cream in a small saucepan and bring to a simmer over medium heat.
3. Pour the cream over the chocolate and let the mixture rest for 1 minute.
4. Gently whisk the mixture until thoroughly combined. Use immediately if drizzling over cookies. Let the ganache cool for 2 hours if piping. The ganache will keep in the refrigerator for up to 5 days.

COATING CHOCOLATE

YIELD: 1 Cup
ACTIVE TIME: 10 Minutes
TOTAL TIME: 10 Minutes

½ lb. chocolate

½ cup coconut oil

½ teaspoon pure vanilla extract

⅛ teaspoon table salt

1. Combine all of the ingredients in a small saucepan and warm over low heat.
2. Stir continually until the chocolate has melted and the mixture is smooth. Use immediately.

CREAM CHEESE FROSTING

YIELD: 3 Cups
ACTIVE TIME: 10 Minutes
TOTAL TIME: 10 Minutes

1 cup unsalted butter, softened

1 cup cream cheese, softened

2 lbs. confectioners' sugar

⅛ teaspoon table salt

¼ cup heavy cream

½ teaspoon pure vanilla extract

1. In the work bowl of a stand mixer fitted with the paddle attachment, combine the butter, cream cheese, confectioners' sugar, and salt and beat on low speed until the sugar starts to be incorporated into the butter. Raise the speed to high and beat until the mixture is smooth and fluffy, 2 to 3 minutes, scraping down the work bowl as necessary.
2. Reduce the speed to low, add the heavy cream and vanilla, and beat to incorporate. Use immediately, or store in the refrigerator for up to 2 weeks. If refrigerating, return to room temperature before using.

SALTED TOFFEE

YIELD: 2 Cups
ACTIVE TIME: 10 Minutes
TOTAL TIME: 10 Minutes

1 cup sugar

½ cup unsalted butter, cubed

½ cup heavy cream

¾ teaspoon table salt

1. Place the sugar in a saucepan and warm it over medium heat, stirring occasionally, until the sugar has melted. Cook until the sugar is amber in color.
2. Add the butter one piece at a time and stir until incorporated. Slowly drizzle in the cream, taking great care as the mixture will spatter.
3. Boil for 1 minute and then remove the pan from heat. Stir in the salt and set the toffee aside to cool and thicken.

ROYAL ICING

YIELD: 3 Cups
ACTIVE TIME: 5 Minutes
TOTAL TIME: 5 Minutes

6 egg whites

1 teaspoon pure vanilla extract

2 lbs. confectioners' sugar

2 drops of gel food coloring (optional)

1. Place the egg whites, vanilla, and confectioners' sugar in a mixing bowl and whisk until the mixture is smooth.
2. If desired, add food coloring. If using immediately, place the icing in a piping bag. If making ahead of time, store it in the refrigerator, where it will keep for 5 days.

YIELD: 4 Cups
ACTIVE TIME: 10 Minutes
TOTAL TIME: 10 Minutes

BUTTERFLUFF FILLING

½ lb. marshmallow creme

1¼ cups unsalted butter, softened

2¾ cups confectioners' sugar

1½ teaspoons pure vanilla extract

¾ teaspoon table salt

1. In the work bowl of a stand mixer fitted with the paddle attachment, cream the marshmallow creme and butter on medium speed until the mixture is very light and fluffy, 2 to 3 minutes, scraping down the work bowl as necessary.
2. Add the confectioners' sugar, vanilla, and salt, reduce the speed to low, and beat for 2 minutes. Use immediately or store in the refrigerator for up to 1 month.

YIELD: 2 Cups
ACTIVE TIME: 15 Minutes
TOTAL TIME: 1 Hour and 30 Minutes

CARAMEL SAUCE

1 cup sugar

¼ cup water

½ cup heavy cream

6 tablespoons unsalted butter, softened

½ teaspoon table salt

½ teaspoon pure vanilla extract

1. Place the sugar and water in a small saucepan and bring to a boil over high heat. Resist the urge to whisk the mixture; instead, swirl the pan occasionally.
2. Once the mixture turns a dark amber color, turn off the heat and, whisking slowly, drizzle in the heavy cream. Be careful, as the mixture may spatter.
3. When all of the cream has been incorporated, add the butter, salt, and vanilla and whisk until smooth. Pour the hot caramel into Mason jars to cool. The caramel sauce can be stored for 1 week at room temperature.

YIELD: ¾ Cup

ACTIVE TIME: 5 Minutes

TOTAL TIME: 5 Minutes

ROQUEFORT CREAM

⅔ cup crumbled Roquefort cheese

2 tablespoons heavy cream, plus more as needed

Pinch of table salt

1. Place all of the ingredients in the work bowl of a stand mixer fitted with the paddle attachment and beat on medium speed until the mixture is smooth and pipeable. If the mixture is still a bit too stiff, incorporate more cream until it has the desired texture.

YIELD: ½ Cups

ACTIVE TIME: 20 Minutes

TOTAL TIME: 3 Hours and 30 Minutes

DULCE DE LECHE

1 (14 oz.) can of sweetened condensed milk

1. Remove the wrapper from the can of condensed milk. Bring a small pot of water to a boil and carefully place the can into the water, making sure the can is completely submerged.
2. Boil for 1½ hours, adding water as necessary. Carefully remove the can from the water, turn it over, and return it to the water. Return to a boil, and boil for an additional 1½ hours.
3. Remove the can from the water and let it cool to room temperature. Open the can and scoop the dulce de leche into an airtight container. Use immediately or store in the refrigerator.

PISTO

YIELD: ¼ Cup
ACTIVE TIME: 5 Minutes
TOTAL TIME: 5 Minutes

4 teaspoons cinnamon

2 teaspoons coriander

2 teaspoons black pepper

2 teaspoons freshly grated nutmeg

1 teaspoon ground cloves

½ teaspoon ground star anise

1. Place all of the ingredients in a bowl, stir to combine, and use immediately or store in an airtight container.

CARAMELIZED WHITE CHOCOLATE

YIELD: 1 Cup
ACTIVE TIME: 25 Minutes
TOTAL TIME: 1 Hour and 30 Minutes

1 lb. white chocolate

Pinch of table salt

2 tablespoons canola oil

1. Preheat the oven to 250°F. Line a rimmed 13 x 18–inch sheet pan with a silicone mat. Chop the white chocolate into small pieces and spread them over the pan. Add the salt and canola oil and stir to coat the chocolate pieces. Place the pan in the oven and bake for 10 minutes.
2. Use a rubber spatula to spread the melting chocolate until it covers the entire pan. Place the pan back in the oven and bake until the white chocolate has caramelized to a deep golden brown, about 30 to 50 minutes, removing to stir every 10 minutes.
3. Carefully pour the caramelized white chocolate into a heatproof container. Use immediately or store at room temperature for up to 1 month.

YIELD: 2 Cups
ACTIVE TIME: 5 Minutes
TOTAL TIME: 5 Minutes

WHIPPED CREAM

2 cups heavy cream

3 tablespoons sugar

1 teaspoon pure vanilla extract

1. In the work bowl of a stand mixer fitted with the whisk attachment, whip the heavy cream, sugar, and vanilla on high until the mixture holds soft peaks.
2. Use immediately or store in the refrigerator for up to 3 days.

YIELD: 2 Cups
ACTIVE TIME: 10 Minutes
TOTAL TIME: 10 Minutes

STREUSEL TOPPING

1 cup plus 2 tablespoons all-purpose flour

½ cup sugar

½ cup light brown sugar

½ cup rolled oats

1 teaspoon cinnamon

½ teaspoon table salt

½ cup unsalted butter, chilled and divided into tablespoons

1. In the work bowl of a stand mixer fitted with the paddle attachment, beat the flour, sugar, brown sugar, oats, cinnamon, and salt on low speed until combined.
2. Turn off the mixer and add the butter. Raise the speed to medium and beat the mixture until the mixture is crumbly and the butter has been absorbed by the dry ingredients, making sure not to overwork the mixture. Use immediately or store in the refrigerator for up to 1 week.

YIELD: 4 Cups
ACTIVE TIME: 30 Minutes
TOTAL TIME: 24 Hours

GIANDUJA CRÉMEUX

2 sheets of silver gelatin

¾ lb. gianduja chocolate, chopped

¼ cup sugar

4 egg yolks

¾ cup whole milk

¾ cup heavy cream

1. Place the gelatin sheets in a small bowl. Add 1 cup of ice and enough cold water that the sheets are completely covered. Let the gelatin bloom.

2. Place the chocolate in a heatproof bowl. Place half of the sugar and the egg yolks in a small bowl and whisk for 2 minutes. Set the mixture aside.

3. In a small saucepan, combine the milk, heavy cream, and remaining sugar and bring to a simmer over medium heat. Slowly pour half of the hot milk mixture into the egg mixture and whisk to incorporate. Pour the tempered egg mixture into the saucepan. Cook, stirring continually, until the mixture thickens and is about to come to a full simmer. Remove the pan from heat.

4. Remove the bloomed gelatin from the ice water. Squeeze to remove as much water as possible from the sheets. Add the sheets to the hot milk mixture base and whisk until they have completely dissolved.

5. Pour the hot milk mixture over the chocolate and let the mixture sit for 1 minute. Whisk to combine, transfer to a heatproof container, and let it cool to room temperature.

6. Store in the refrigerator overnight before using.

CONVERSION TABLE

WEIGHTS

1 oz. = 28 grams
2 oz. = 57 grams
4 oz. (¼ lb.) = 113 grams
8 oz. (½ lb.) = 227 grams
16 oz. (1 lb.) = 454 grams

VOLUME MEASURES

⅛ teaspoon = 0.6 ml
¼ teaspoon = 1.23 ml
½ teaspoon = 2.5 ml
1 teaspoon = 5 ml
1 tablespoon (3 teaspoons) = ½ fluid oz. = 15 ml
2 tablespoons = 1 fluid oz. = 29.5 ml
¼ cup (4 tablespoons) = 2 fluid oz. = 59 ml
⅓ cup (5⅓ tablespoons) = 2.7 fluid oz. = 80 ml
½ cup (8 tablespoons) = 4 fluid oz. = 120 ml
⅔ cup (10⅔ tablespoons) = 5.4 fluid oz. = 160 ml
¾ cup (12 tablespoons) = 6 fluid oz. = 180 ml
1 cup (16 tablespoons) = 8 fluid oz. = 240 ml

TEMPERATURE EQUIVALENTS

°F	°C	Gas Mark
225	110	¼
250	130	½
275	140	1
300	150	2
325	170	3
350	180	4
375	190	5
400	200	6
425	220	7
450	230	8
475	240	9
500	250	10

LENGTH MEASURES

1⁄16 inch = 1.6 mm
⅛ inch = 3 mm
¼ inch = 6.35 mm
½ inch = 1.25 cm
¾ inch = 2 cm
1 inch = 2.5 cm

INDEX

B

C

D

M

N

O

P

Q

R

S

T

V

W

X

About Cider Mill Press Book Publishers

Good ideas ripen with time. From seed to harvest, Cider Mill Press brings fine reading, information, and entertainment together between the covers of its creatively crafted books. Our Cider Mill bears fruit twice a year, publishing a new crop of titles each spring and fall.

"Where Good Books Are Ready for Press"

501 Nelson Place
Nashville, Tennessee 37214

cidermillpress.com